Christmas

The Annual of Christmas Literature and Art

Christmas

Christmas

The Annual of Christmas Literature and Art

Volume Fifty-nine

Augsburg Fortress, Minneapolis

In this volume

A continuing goal of CHRISTMAS is to seek out and to celebrate the many Christmas traditions that have come from other lands and taken root in the United States. A growing number of our population claims an Hispanic heritage, whether from Mexico, South and Central America, or the Caribbean. A sampling from this rich culture is offered here.

The heart of all Christmas celebration, of course, is the timeless story of Christ's birth, which is beautifully illustrated for us by California artist John August Swanson, son of a Mexican mother and a Swedish father. His work hangs in such prestigious galleries as the Smithsonian, the Tate Gallery in London, the Bibliothèque Nationale in Paris, and the Vatican Museum.

Two articles, "A San Antonio Christmas" and "Season of Joy in Mexico," capture the blend of devotion and festivity that make Christmastime in these communities unique. "Christmas Celebrations in South America" presents the customs of five other countries.

Acknowledging the importance of music in any Hispanic Christmas celebration and the importance of the guitar in Hispanic music, five carols appear in both Spanish and English, preceded by an article on the development of the guitar.

In "Adoration of the Shepherds" Phillip Gugel explores the fascinating painting by Spanish master El Greco, thus rounding out our tribute to the Hispanic community.

Seasoned readers of CHRISTMAS, as well as first-time readers, will welcome the return of artist Bob Artley. His captivating look back to yesteryear in "Toys Father Made" will delight young and old alike.

We regret the absence of another CHRISTMAS favorite, "Christmas Corners" by cartoonist Graham Hunter, who died last year. His amusing portrayals of familiar yuletide situations appeared in the last six issues.

Nonetheless, this issue offers much good seasonal reading, including three new short stories. May it only serve to enrich for you this already precious, holy season.

Table of Contents

Editorial staff: Gloria E. Bengtson, director; Jennifer Huber, editor; Sandra Gangelhoff, assistant editor; Richard Hillert, music consultant.

The Christmas Story

According to St. Luke and St. Matthew

Now in the sixth month the angel Gabriel was sent by God to a city of Galilee named Nazareth, to a virgin betrothed to a man whose name was Joseph, of the house of David. The virgin's name was Mary.

And having come in, the angel said to her, "Rejoice, highly favored one, the Lord is with you; blessed are you among women!"

But when she saw him, she was troubled at his saying, and considered what manner of greeting this was.

Then the angel said to her, "Do not be afraid, Mary, for you have found favor with God. And behold, you will conceive in your womb and bring forth a Son, and shall call his name Jesus. He will be great, and will be called the Son of the Highest; and the Lord God will give him the throne of his father David.

And he will reign over the house of Jacob forever, and of his kingdom there will be no end."

Then Mary said to the angel, "How can this be, since I do not know a man?"

And the angel answered and said to her, "The Holy Spirit will come upon you, and the power of the Highest will overshadow you; therefore, also, that Holy One who is to be born will be called the Son of God.

"Now indeed, Elizabeth your relative has also conceived a son in her old age; and this is now the sixth month for her who was called barren. For with God nothing will be impossible."

Then Mary said, "Behold the maidservant of the Lord! Let it be to me according to your word." And the angel departed from her.

And it came to pass in those days that a decree went out from Caesar Augustus that all the world should be registered. This census first took place while Quirinius was governing Syria. So all went to be registered, everyone to his own city.

And Joseph also went up from Galilee, out of the city of Nazareth, into Judea, to the city of David, which is called Bethlehem, because he was of the house and lineage of David, to be registered with Mary, his betrothed wife, who was with child.

So it was, that while they were there, the days were completed for her to be delivered.

And she brought forth her firstborn Son, and wrapped him in swaddling cloths, and laid him in a manger, because there was no room for them in the inn.

Now there were in the same country shepherds living out in the fields, keeping watch over their flock by night. And behold, an angel of the Lord stood before them, and the glory of the Lord shone around them, and they were greatly afraid.

Then the angel said to them, "Do not be afraid, for behold, I bring you good tidings of great joy which will be to all people. For there is born to you this day in the city of David a Savior, who is Christ the Lord. And this will be the sign to you: You will find a babe wrapped in swaddling cloths, lying in a manger."

And suddenly there was with the angel a multitude of the heavenly host praising God and saying:

"Glory to God in the highest,
And on earth peace, good will
        toward men!"

So it was, when the angels had gone away from them into heaven, that the shepherds said to one another, "Let us now go to Bethlehem and see this thing that has come to pass, which the Lord has made known to us."

And they came with haste and found Mary and Joseph, and the babe lying in a manger. Now when they had seen him, they made widely known the saying which was told them concerning this child. And all those who heard it marveled at those things which were told them by the shepherds. But Mary kept all these things and pondered them in her heart. Then the shepherds returned, glorifying and praising God for all the things that they had heard and seen, as it was told them.

Now after Jesus was born in Bethlehem of Judea in the days of Herod the king, behold, wise men from the East came to Jerusalem, saying, "Where is he who has been born King of the Jews? For we have seen his star in the East and have come to worship him."

When Herod the king heard these things, he was troubled, and all Jerusalem with him. And when he had gathered all the chief priests and scribes of the people together, he inquired of them where the Christ was to be born.

So they said to him, "In Bethlehem of Judea, for thus it is written by the prophet:

*But you, Bethlehem, in the land
    of Judah,
Are not the least among the rulers
    of Judah;
For out of you shall come a Ruler
Who will shepherd my people Israel."*

Then Herod, when he had secretly called the wise men, determined from them what time the star appeared. And he sent them to Bethlehem and said, "Go and search diligently for the young child, and when you have found him, bring back word to me, that I may come and worship him also."

When they heard the king, they departed; and behold, the star which they had seen in the East went before them, till it came and stood over where the young child was. When they saw the star, they rejoiced with exceedingly great joy. And when they had come into the house, they saw the young child with Mary his mother, and fell down and worshiped him. And when they had opened their treasures, they presented gifts to him: gold, frankincense, and myrrh.

Then being divinely warned in a dream that they should not return to Herod, they departed for their own country another way.

Now when they had departed, behold, an angel of the Lord appeared to Joseph in a dream, saying, "Arise, take the young child and his mother, flee to Egypt, and stay there until I bring you word; for Herod will seek the young child to destroy him."

When he arose, he took the young child and his mother by night and departed for Egypt, and was there until the death of Herod, that it might be fulfilled which was spoken by the Lord through the prophet, saying, *"Out of Egypt I called my Son."*

But when Herod was dead, behold, an angel of the Lord appeared in a dream to Joseph in Egypt, saying, "Arise, take the young child and his mother, and go to the land of Israel, for those who sought the young child's life are dead."

Then he arose, took the young child and his mother, and came into the land of Israel. But when he heard that Archelaus was reigning over Judea instead of his father Herod, he was afraid to go there. And being warned by God in a dream, he turned aside into the region of Galilee.

And he came and dwelt in a city called Nazareth, that it might be fulfilled which was spoken by the prophets, *"He shall be called a Nazarene."*

A San Antonio Christmas

CANDACE LESLIE

Christmas lights in giant oak trees reflect on the water along the winding *Paseo del Rio*. The river banks glow with thousands of candles. Mariachis (Mexican street bands) play *"Feliz Navidad"* from barges cruising slowly down the sparkling waterway. Pancho Claus, wearing a black beard and a bright serape, greets the children and other passersby. Handwoven straw wreaths twined with red and green hang on doors of shops and houses. Suspended high above the city, like a giant sombrero, the Tower of the Americas glows with colored lights.

As in most cities, the stores are bulging with toys and gifts and bustling with excited children and weary shoppers. But in San Antonio, Texas, there is a difference. From early Advent through Christmas Day and well into Epiphany, the Hispanic people of this southwestern city tell and retell the stories of the season in their churches, backyards, and homes for the benefit and delight of families and friends. Their colorful traditions—some rooted in Spain, some rooted in Mexico—have also become a part of the city's public celebrations. For both the visitor to San Antonio and for the city's residents, opportunities abound to share in the richness of Hispanic faith and festivity.

In 1718, the Viceroy of Spain founded San Antonio as a fortress with an accompanying mission, *San Antonio de Valero*, which would one day be known as "The Alamo." While many other cultural and ethnic groups would eventually settle in this key city of the southwest, none would provide a richer heritage than those of Spanish and Mexican descent. From the restored little village, *La Villita*, to the Spanish Governor's Palace, from the chain of missions to San Fernando Cathedral, from Market Square to charming side-street restaurants, Hispanic influence abounds throughout the whole city. A wise and visionary Conservation Society, with the assistance of city leaders, churches, and other groups, works to keep this native culture alive. This is especially true during the Christmas season.

Celebrations begin the weekend following Thanksgiving, when the lights along the downtown riverwalk, the *Paseo del Rio*, are turned on for the first time and a parade of gaily lighted barges, filled with music and festivity, travel the winding waterway. Every night until the New Year the lights will shine, delighting the crowds that come to join in a host of special celebrations, to visit the assorted shops and restaurants, or just to stroll beside the sparkling water.

Fiesta Navidena

At Market Square, located on the site of San Antonio's first official public market, *Fiesta Navidena* fills three colorful days early in December with the music and festivities of Christmas. Mexican folk dancers perform in bright costumes, mariachis delight the ear with trumpets and guitars, the aroma of tamales and spiced hot chocolate and other traditional Christmas foods fills the air. At the center of Market Square, *El Mercado*, a large indoor area patterned after an authentic Mexican market, draws thousands of shoppers who manage to find gifts for almost everyone on their Christmas lists from the tremendous assortment of curios, clothes, and crafts imported from south of the border.

On the Saturday of *Fiesta Navidena*, children and adults alike bring their favorite animals to Market Square for a traditional ceremony, The Blessing of the Pets. Many believe this ceremony is especially fitting during the Advent season because of the significant role the animals played on the night of Christ's birth. A donkey carried Mary to the stable; perhaps lambs and sheep accompanied the shepherds who came to worship the child; the Magi rode camels on their long journey; and the beasts themselves shared their warm room and the manger with the holy family. In honor of the animals' Christmas role, a small boy may bring his goat or a little girl her kitten and join the crowd of animal lovers and their

Every night from the weekend following Thanksgiving until the New Year the lights along the downtown riverwalk will shine, creating a beautiful scene for the Christmas festivities. Luminarias, lit candles in paper sacks, line the walkways.

(left) Adults and children bring their favorite animals to Market Square to be blessed by the Bishop of the Archdiocese of San Antonio in the traditional ceremony known as *The Blessing of the Pets.*

(below) El Mercado, an indoor shopping area modeled after an authentic Mexican market, draws thousands of shoppers with its curios, clothes, and crafts.

holy family's long-ago search for lodging. Sponsored by the San Antonio Conservation Society, this lovely candlelit musical ceremony known as *Las Posadas* or The Inns is a shortened presentation of a traditional Mexican celebration still observed in many local communities and neighborhoods. In this version, designed for visitors and citizens alike, Mary and Joseph and the Angel Gabriel set out along the *Paseo del Rio.* At the head of the procession, *El Misterio,* the baby Jesus, is carried reverently on a litter. Behind come the faithful, their candles glowing and their sung litanies and hymns filling the air. Spectators often join in along the way, having been provided with candles and songsheets so they, too, can take part, even if Spanish is not their language.

Several times the holy family and their followers stop to ask in song for a place to rest. Each time they are answered by a choir singing from one of the stone bridges arching the river. "There is no room here," the singers tell them. "You must go on." Slowly they continue, followed by the faithful and observed by the hundreds of spectators who throng the walkways or cruise the river in a fleet of boats and barges. At last they reach *La Villita,* where they are welcomed by more crowds and a priest. The figure of the infant Jesus is placed in a creche, and

pets, many bedecked with bright Christmas bows for the special occasion. Strolling among them, the Bishop of the Archdiocese of San Antonio asks God's blessing on all creatures, large and small.

Pancho Claus visits Market Square this day, too. His hat is a broad-brimmed sombrero. A bright red serape covers his shoulders. His beard is full and black. But like his familiar white-bearded cousin, he carries a bag of treats to share with the children as he listens to their Christmas requests, laughing heartily and wishing each a *"Feliz Navidad."*

Fiesta de las Luminarias

On the first two weekends in December, the *Paseo del Rio,* San Antonio's riverwalk, takes on an added beauty with the lighting of thousands of candles placed in paper sacks partially filled with sand. This *Fiesta de las Luminarias* follows a tradition probably begun in the 1500s and represents the lighting of the holy family's way to Bethlehem. As with all the city's Hispanic Christmas traditions, it is accompanied by stories, legends, and interpretations that have been handed down through the centuries. Some say the little candles or *velitas* are rays of love, hope, and peace; the sand, some say, represents the sands of time. Whatever their meaning, the lovely flickering lights create an inviting pathway for river-strollers to follow.

Las Posadas

On the second weekend of the *Fiesta de las Luminarias,* a young man and woman, portraying Mary and Joseph, travel the candlelit path in a reenactment of the

Los Posadas (The Inns) reenacts the holy family's search for lodging in Bethlehem. The players ask in song for a resting place and are answered by a choir. Spectators are provided with candles and songsheets so they may join in.

traditionally enacted on each of the nine days before Christmas, are a novena or nine days devotion in honor of the nine months that Mary carried Jesus in her womb. Such dramatizations were a favorite medium of the missionaries for bringing Christian stories and Christian values to life for the inhabitants of the New World. Many of the dramatizations have survived the centuries and today are carried out in a variety of ways, such as the popular shortened version of *Las Posadas* presented along the *Paseo del Rio*. They still serve to heighten awareness of the true meanings of Christmas.

Los Pastores

Also rooted deeply in the past, *Los Pastores* (The Shepherds), embodies a commitment to heritage and faith by both the Hispanic people and the Conservation Society of San Antonio. A folkdrama presenting the story of the shepherds' journey to Bethlehem, *Los Pastores*, like *Las Posadas*, is enacted both in close-knit neighborhoods and in public performances. Also believed to have been used by missionaries to teach biblical stories and messages, the origins of this centuries-old drama lie lost in the past. It has been classified by scholars as everything from a folkplay to a great work of literature to a simple expression of a faithful people. Some think *Los Pastores*, in its various versions and interpretations, may have been performed in San Antonio at least 25,000 times, in churches, backyards, schools, or wherever the performers were invited.

Each year, on a January weekend early in Epiphany, the Guadalupe Players present one or two special performances of *Los Pastores* for the general public to enjoy. Presented at Mission San Jose, an eighteenth-century mission which is both a parish church and a National Park, this *pastorela* (shepherds' play) is sponsored by the San Antonio Conservation Society. The actors and actresses are the same farmers, business folk, and young people who will give at least two dozen more performances in backyards and churches and halls before the season of Epiphany ends. The players rehearse for weeks, learning the long speeches and songs that have been handed down through the centuries. Some are playing parts once enacted by parents or grandparents and which they hope, one day, their own children will inherit.

Though many *pastorelas* last five hours or more, this presentation runs only half that time. Held out-of-doors with the lovely stone facade of the mission as a backdrop, both the staging and the story are simple. At one end of an open space called a "corral" stands Inferno, decorated with ferocious paintings of demons. Here dwell Lucifer and his clan, including Satan. Eighty feet away the humble stable houses Mary and Joseph and the infant Jesus. Between the two, the shepherds gather and, on hearing the news of the Messiah's birth from an angel, begin their journey to Bethlehem.

the weary travelers find rest. Everyone sings songs of welcome and thanksgiving, bells ring, prayers are said.

Excitement mounts as the children sing the traditional request for a *piñata* and everyone moves to the plaza for cookies and hot chocolate. Here mariachis again play their trumpets and guitars and sing traditional Mexican songs. Colorful dancers add brilliance and movement to the night. And, as the children had hoped, the colorful, comical *piñata* hangs high above their heads, waiting to rain its shower of treats onto the eager players.

Piñatas

Piñatas are always a part of *Las Posadas*, and of many other Christmas festivities as well. A gaily decorated figure made of clay or papier mâché and filled with candy and treats, the *piñata* is usually hung from a tree branch with a rope attached to maneuver it up and down. The figure might be an animal, a watermelon, a basket, or even, in these modern times, a car or a rocket. Children, wearing blindfolds, take turns hitting at the *piñata* with a stick while the crowd shouts advice and directions. When a well-directed blow cracks the *piñata* open at last, the children, screaming and shouting, scurry for the shower of candy and goodies.

Like many Hispanic traditions, the *piñata* also claims its share of legends. Some say the *piñata* was introduced by Franciscan missionaries in Mexico, to be a representation of the devil. Because this wicked and elusive enemy is always invisible, participants wear blindfolds as they strike against evil with the "rod of virtue." Those who persevere to the end are showered with God's blessings. While children probably are unaware of this weighty message as they excitedly strive for the rewards of the *piñata*, the story reminds one that many of the southwestern Hispanic Christmas traditions are rooted in the Spanish missionaries' early attempts to explain the Christian message to the people of the New World.

Las Posadas, for example, of Augustinian origin and

(right) Los Pastores (The Shepherds) is a folk drama presenting the story of the shepherds' journey to Bethlehem. Each year the Guadalupe Players present one or two special public performances at the Mission San Jose.

(below) Piñatas filled with candy and treats are a favorite part of the Christmas festivities. Children take turns trying to break the piñata.

They wear costumes of their own creation, combinations of cowboy garb, colorful regalia, and traditional biblical illustration. Their crooks, embellished with bells and tinsel, provide accompaniment for the Gregorian-folk-Mexican songs they sing along the way.

A narrator keeps the non-Spanish speakers in the audience informed of the shepherds' progress and of the numerous battles and struggles between good and evil, the latter represented by the host of demons dressed in brilliant handmade cloaks decorated with symbolic designs. For the players, *Los Pastores* is both a religious activity and a heavy commitment. Besides designing and making their own costumes, they rehearse and perform their roles for many weeks.

Once under way, a performance is never cancelled, no matter how the weather deteriorates, for the drama must be completed—good must always triumph over evil. Sometimes Mary and Joseph, waiting patiently in the outdoor stable, wrap themselves in blankets and sip hot drinks to stay the bitter cold of the January night. But they will never leave their post until the shepherds have arrived to pay homage to the child who lies in the manger.

Despite the seriousness of its message, *Los Pastores* is not a weighty event. Occasionally players chat with friends in the crowd, or make subtle jokes and comments. A little devil plays tricks on the old hermit who accompanies the shepherds on their journey. One of the travelers is lazy and must be prodded. Another prepares meals of roast kid and *tortillas*. Audience members often huddle in blankets and sleeping bags to keep warm, or gather around roaring barrel-fires, or fill up on steaming tamales and hot chocolate. There is much laughter. And there is much devotion, especially when, at last, the shepherds reach their destination. Everyone, including Lucifer and his entourage, as well as any of the spectators who wish, offers homage to the child with kisses and tiny gifts. Once again the goodness of God triumphs over all the schemes and plots of evil. The message of Christmas has not been overcome.

In addition to the annual events of San Antonio's very long Christmas season, individual churches and neighborhoods of the Hispanic communities often celebrate the season with special services or events to which the public is invited. Arts and crafts shows, sales of traditional Christmas foods, concerts and programs often highlight the season. Because these vary from year to year, anyone who wishes to learn about special events should contact the Convention and Visitors Bureau in late November or early December for specific information.

But wherever one goes in this city, the Hispanic influence is felt. Its rich traditions are present in the activities of the season and in the people who participate in them. And this is especially so at this lovely time of year, when the devout celebrate the birth of Christ.

Pablo's Paradura Party

KATHARINE VAN ETTEN LYFORD

"ARE YOU SURE?" asked Diego, crawling behind the high hedge of scarlet poinsettias to join his friend.

"*Si, si,*" whispered Tony, "I just looked through the window."

"And you're certain nobody is inside the house who might see us?" Diego was still doubtful.

Tony protested impatiently, "It's like I told you before. Pablo's father is out of town and his uncle is taking Pablo to Pico Peak for a New Year's treat. There they go now!" He pointed to the steep slope at the end of the street where a cable car inched its way from the sunny flower gardens of Merida to snow-covered Venezuelan mountains. "Lucky guy! He told me he was off for some fun and would leave the work to us."

"What did he mean by that?" asked Diego, scowling at his friend.

"Just one of his silly jokes, I guess," answered Tony. Then pushing Diego flat to the ground he whispered, "Down! Here comes Pablo's mother."

A slender, dark-haired young woman left the house and started along the street. As she turned the corner, Tony gave a sigh of relief. Then he chuckled, "It's OK now. We can thank my mother for getting her out of the way by asking her over to our house to see the new television set we got for Christmas." Beckoning Diego to follow, he slipped from the protecting poinsettias and ran toward the open front door of the house.

Once inside the boys found the sitting room still festive with Christmas decorations. The *pesebre* (manger scene) filled one big corner with its figures of the holy family, surrounded by worshiping angels, shepherds, and cattle. Close by were the three Magi cleverly carved of Venezuelan balsa wood and clothed in royal robes of purple, red, and blue paint. Every night since *Noche Buena* (Christmas Eve) they had been moved forward a little from the cardboard background representing the five White Eagle snowpeaks of Merida. On January 6, the three kings would be placed directly in front of the Christ child's crib.

But what would they find? An empty bed of straw. For Tony was lifting the babe of Bethlehem from the manger. Turning to Diego, he exclaimed, "Imagine old Pablo leaving *El Niño* (the Child) lying down on New Year's Day."

Both boys shook their heads in amazement. How could their playmate have forgotten a Christmas custom as old as the ancient Venezuelan city in which they lived? Everybody in Merida knew that the Christ child in each crib must welcome the New Year standing up and remain standing until the feast of Candelaria in February. For *El Niño* was no ordinary baby and all good *Méredeños* cherished the legend of how the precocious Christ child proved this by standing up when he was only a week old. According to local custom anyone failing so to honor *El Niño* could expect to be punished by having the figure secretly stolen and hidden away. The only way to retrieve the missing *El Niño* was to give a Paradura party to search for it and bring it back home.

Wrapping the figure of the baby Christ in a handkerchief, Tony tucked it inside his jacket. Then, with Diego scouting to make sure no one saw them, the boys left the house to hide once more behind the poinsettias. There they began to make plans.

"Aunt Yolanda says she will keep the baby hidden for us," Tony confided in a low voice. "She will make him new clothes and be a good parent, too, if we ask her." He paused, then asked, "But who will be chief godfather and plan the procession?"

"Pablo is sure to ask his Uncle Carlos," replied Diego, "because he can get all the firecrackers and sparklers right in his store."

Tony nodded, "And I'll bet he asks the school teacher and his wife to be the godparents and hold the other corners of the handkerchief to carry *El Niño*."

For an hour the boys lay low talking about the Paradura party their schoolmate would have to give to insure the return of the Christ child to the manger. Every now and then Diego sputtered, "Mighty queer that Pablo forgot to stand him up on New Year's Day. He's usually so sharp about getting ahead of us. Won't he be mad when he gets home and finds his crib is empty!"

But Pablo wasn't mad. To the surprise of his friends, he quickly admitted his error, then plunged enthusiastically into preparations for the Paradura party that he and his parents would give. He even coached Diego's three-year-old sister in the part she would play.

Everybody knew that the Christ child must welcome the new year standing up and remain so until Candelaria.

The evening of the party arrived. Uncle Carlos as chief godparent lined up the guests as they arrived at Pablo's home. At the head of the procession he put two small heralds armed with firecrackers and sparklers to signal the approach of those seeking the lost babe of Bethlehem. Next marched the musicians, their *maracas*, *furrucos*, and *cuatros* ready to play as soon as the baby was found. Behind them marched Diego's small sister, proudly carrying a large cardboard star and leading the way for two teenagers dressed as Mary and Joseph. Wearing brightly colored blankets and paper crowns, Tony, Diego and another classmate represented the Magi. Behind them walked the godparents carrying a large silk handkerchief.

At a word from Uncle Carlos, all the marchers lighted their candles and surged forward singing:

Here we come to search for the child
Who has been taken from his home.
Here we come, shepherds, here we come,
Here we come all together.

The candlelit cobblestone streets echoed with the traditional carol as the colorful procession wound its way toward Tony's house. Although he and Diego had tried to keep the hiding place secret, word had leaked out and the whereabouts of *El Niño* were all too well-known. So, when the godparents knocked on the door, Aunt Yolanda appeared carrying the figure dressed in brand-new clothes for the party in his honor and the trip back to his crib.

Solemnly the godparents placed the little figure in the center of the big silk handkerchief. With the musicians striking up the traditional tune, the marchers started the return trip singing:

Here we have found the child
Whom we thought was lost.
Now we shall take him home
And his godparents shall carry him.

Chanting the many verses of this familiar holiday song, the candlelit procession wended its way through the narrow streets. Arriving at Pablo's home, they found Pablo and his parents at the open door eager to welcome *El Niño* and his caroling escorts.

Also standing in the doorway, Uncle Carlos lifted the figure from the handkerchief held by the godparents and held it out so that all the guests could salute the babe of Bethlehem. Then, with the godparents beside him, he walked inside the house to the manger and placed the little figure back in the straw, this time standing up. The guests gathered close and sang:

As we give this kiss
To the blessed child Jesus
The godparents will stand him up
And he will remain standing.

Toward the end of the carol, the younger children crowded close to the crib impatient to begin the gift-giving, their part in the Paradura party. A chubby five-year-old pushed forward and held out a rumpled package, reciting in a frightened squeak:

I am a little shepherd
Who comes from Bailadores
And I bring the Christ child
This pack of voladores *(firecrackers).*

Placing his present at the feet of *El Niño*, the little boy stepped back to make room for other small guests. Uncle Carlos and the godparents helped Pablo make sure that every child had a chance to recite a poem and present a gift. Among the last was Diego's small sister. Still carrying her paper star, she offered the Christ child a present wrapped in well-worn wax paper. With one chubby finger in her dimpled mouth she shyly whispered the words Pablo had taught her:

I am a poor gypsy
Who comes from Japan
To offer the child
This tortilla of ham.

While other guests laughed and clapped, Pablo lifted the timid *señorita* to his shoulder and led the way to the dining room where tables were piled high with cookies and cakes and other good things to eat.

An hour later as Pablo made his way through the push of singing, dancing guests, he beckoned Diego and Tony to join him. Standing by the door he said, *"Muchas gracias* (thanks a lot) for hiding *El Niño."* He chuckled, adding, "You know, I figured you two would be smart enough to take a hint."

Choking on the frosty cookie he was eating, Tony sputtered, "You mean you left your Christ child lying down on New Year's Day on purpose?"

"So we would take it and hide it?" Diego couldn't believe what he was hearing.

"Sure!" smiled Pablo, "If I hadn't left my baby Jesus lying down, how could we have a Paradura party like this?" And he pointed to the room full of happy guests and to *El Niño* safely home and standing up in his crib.

Christmas Customs in South America

LOUISE B. WYLY

IN SOUTH AMERICA, Christmas falls during the warm midsummer season when hot, dry winds (called *zonda*) blow from the north. This weather, combined with the variety of national backgrounds of the people, has given rise to a variety of unique holiday traditions. Some North American and Anglo-Saxon customs have seeped into these countries, but very slowly.

Most of the South American countries have festivities lasting from December 16 to January 6, with singing of Christmas carols and dancing to stringed instruments. Common customs include the *precepio* (manger), the midnight *Misa de Gallo* (Mass of the Cock) on Christmas Eve, and gift-giving on Epiphany or Three Kings Day.

Most people of South America have retained Spanish customs and speak Spanish, with the exception of those in Brazil, where Portuguese is spoken and Germanic customs prevail. Following are some special customs and traditions that do vary from country to country.

Epiphany in Argentina

Festivities in Argentina center around New Year's Day and *Los Reyes Magos* (Three Kings Day or Magi Day on January 6).

Argentinian children write a letter to the Magi requesting certain gifts. Then on the eve of Three Kings Day, the children set their shoes either on the windowsill or beside their beds. Their letter is placed inside one of the shoes. That way, the Magi will know exactly what toys to bring them.

The children eagerly anticipate their gifts and are rarely disappointed since Argentinian parents are usually very generous.

Each family also leaves water and hay outside so the horses or camels of the Magi may eat and be refreshed for the long journey to Jerusalem to see the Christ child.

Three Kings Day, also known as Epiphany or "Manifestation Day" (Greek: *epiphaneia*), celebrates the visit of the Magi when they brought gifts to the Christ child, and fell at his feet in worship.

On this day at teatime, the "Pie of the Magi" is traditionally eaten. This pie is a sweet cake baked in the form of a ring, then covered with sugar and jam, and filled with little gifts.

These activities all add to the joy and happiness of the Argentinian children as they celebrate this festive holiday season.

Trimming the Tree in Brazil

Since 90 percent of Brazil's people are Roman Catholic, much emphasis is placed upon the midnight *Misa de Gallo* (Mass of the Cock). Christmas trees, a result of strong Germanic influence, stand in public places right alongside the *mangedora* (manger scenes) and trimming the Christmas tree provides another highlight of the season.

On Christmas Eve, the Brazilian family gathers to sing German Christmas carols and hymns, the favorite of which is Franz Gruber's "Silent Night."

As the tree is trimmed, the parents tell the Christmas story in words simple enough for even the youngest child to understand.

That night is a special treat for the children, who are allowed to stay up for the reading of the Christmas story from Luke 2. Afterwards the family joins in prayer. Before going to bed, the children place their shoes under the tree for Papa Noel to fill with toys and treats.

Protestant missions have introduced "white gifts" to Brazil. These are gifts of food—perhaps a potato or two, perhaps a little bit of rice—to make a dinner for a poor person. The gifts are wrapped in white paper. During the *Misa de Gallo*, everyone walks to the front of the church to place their gifts beside a crude manger. The manger is filled with straw and a light, symbolizing "The Light of the World." Thus the worshipers express joy in giving—the real meaning of Christmas.

Markets in Peru

During the Christmas season in Peru, people crowd the markets to buy all sorts of toys and delicious foods, which are spread out on mats on the ground.

Indians travel great distances to come to the city in order to build shrines in the churches. Then the Indians stay to shop, adding to the crowd of pushing and shoving shoppers, all eager to buy for the holidays.

By Christmas Eve, their celebrations include much singing, laughing, and dancing. Indians, carrying ice pails on their heads, go gracefully amid the crowds calling, *"Helado! Helado!"* ("Ice!"). The ice stalls also are crowded with people who are eager to cool off on such a hot, sultry night.

At midnight, all quiets down as the cathedral bell strikes, calling everyone to *Misa de Gallo*. The people drop to their knees to pray. When the twelfth stroke has sounded, they rise and wish each other a *Noche Buena* (a good or holy night). Then they proceed to midnight mass. Later, carolers go from house to house singing old Spanish Christmas carols to the accompaniment of castanets and tambourines.

In Lima, capital of Peru and "City of One Hundred Churches," Christmas is a church holiday, yet it must compete with the greatest bullfight of the year. Following the fight, everyone continues to celebrate the holiday in his or her own special way.

The Pesebres in Venezuela

Venezuelans blend a mixed ancestry of both Christian and non-Christian customs. However, in the living room of almost every home in Venezuela, the nativity set with a *nacimiento* (crib) or *pesebre* (manger) is displayed from December 16 to January 6.

Each family creates their own *pesebre*—some simple, others elaborate works of art. In some homes, the *pesebre* becomes an extensive set, including mountains, hills, valleys, all details scaled to reproduce the country of Galilee. Others become a hodgepodge of all sizes, shapes, and colors of figures. However, all the sets include the infant Jesus, Mary, the oxen, the donkey, the shepherds, and the Magi.

During the Christmas season in Venezuela, boys and girls and their parents go from house to house to visit and see other *pesebres*. The figures called *santos* (saints) become treasured family heirlooms and are passed from generation to generation, replaced only when they are beyond repair.

On *Noche Buena* (Christmas Eve), all the children gather at home to celebrate. In Venezuela, children receive gifts on December 25 and on January 6. Many children believe the Christ child brings their gifts on December 25. Others think a little mouse brings gifts. But on Three Kings Day (January 6), Saint Nick is the one they think who leaves presents on their bed.

Masquerading in Colombia

In Colombia, the *Niño Dios* (Christ child) is a central image, and the *pesebre* (Christmas crib) finds a prominent place in the living room of each home.

On Christmas Eve, children gather to sing *villancicos* (old Christmas carols) to guitars and other stringed instruments. But about 9:00 P.M., masqueraders dressed in brightly colored costumes come out of their homes and gather in the streets. This custom is unique to Colombia.

This is the night of *aguinaldos* (Christmas bonuses) and merriment. Everyone tries to recognize a friend or a neighbor, for if they can correctly guess someone's identity, they receive an *aguinaldo* from the person they have recognized.

At midnight, the masqueraders disappear and the towns become quiet. Then church bells peal, calling everyone to midnight mass.

Following the mass, individual families meet to feast on tamales and roast pig or chicken. They also have *bunuelos* for dessert (a deep-fried lemon dough served with powdered sugar and honey). This feasting lasts until morning. Eventually, the children become tired and must go to bed, but not before leaving their shoes on the windowsill for *Niño Dios* to fill with toys and bonbons.

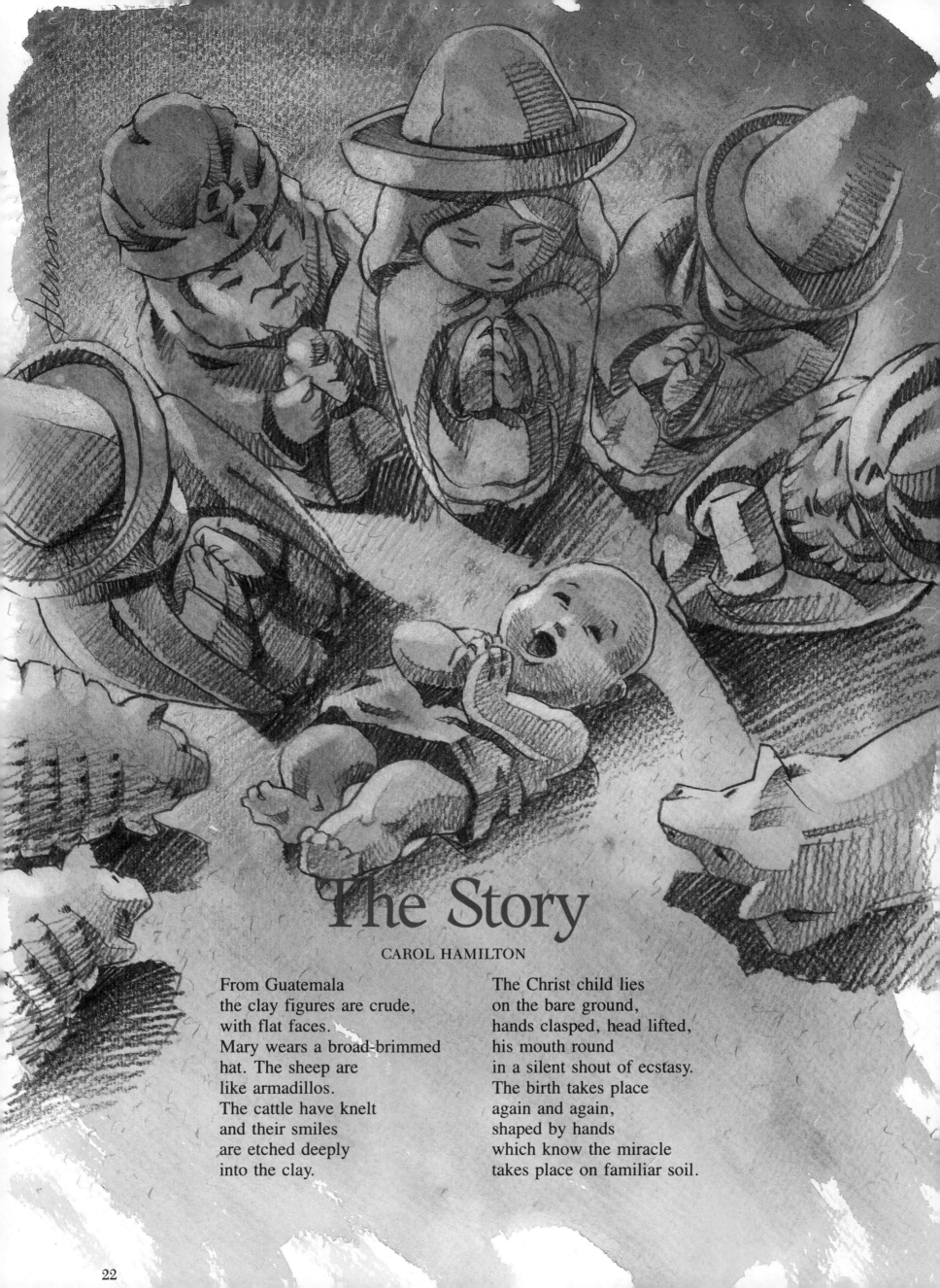

The Story

CAROL HAMILTON

From Guatemala
the clay figures are crude,
with flat faces.
Mary wears a broad-brimmed
hat. The sheep are
like armadillos.
The cattle have knelt
and their smiles
are etched deeply
into the clay.

The Christ child lies
on the bare ground,
hands clasped, head lifted,
his mouth round
in a silent shout of ecstasy.
The birth takes place
again and again,
shaped by hands
which know the miracle
takes place on familiar soil.

The Guitar

Its History and Importance in Hispanic Culture

TONY HAUSER

AT NO OTHER TIME of year does music and singing burst forth in more abundance than at Christmas. Around the world well-loved carols again rise to the lips of those who worship the Christ child, echoing the angels' song to the shepherds. Perhaps the angels chose to sing to humble shepherds, the most common folk of their day, because they knew that music above all can express the deep emotions of the human heart. The angels sang of joy and peace and good will; they sang of hope and of desire satisfied, especially the desire for a Savior and for the redemption of the world. They had a lot to sing about! Down through the ages people, hearing the story of Jesus' birth, have continued to sing. There just is no better way to express the importance of that sacred event.

The song of the angels has inspired such grand music as Handel's *Messiah;* but even more telling is that unique folk culture—the body of

Christmas carols that exists wherever the name of Jesus is known. Nowhere is this more true than in the Hispanic culture, where music and singing go hand-in-hand with the celebration of Christmas. And where you find music and singing you find the guitar, that most favored instrument of the people.

It may truly be said that the guitar is the most popular gift from the Hispanic cultures of Europe and the Americas to the world. The guitar's versatility, portability, and polyphonic (chord playing) abilities contribute to its popularity. It has as many moods as there are people; it may be raucously loud or plaintively sweet. In its many forms it is played by Peruvian Indians, British rock stars, and even Japanese robots. Yet, as we trace the guitar through history, noting its many different constructions and uses, it becomes evident that the Hispanic culture is predominately responsible for the birth and development of the guitar.

When speaking of the guitar one

has to speak of *guitars,* for the family of the guitar is large. There are brothers, sisters, babies, and even a very overweight uncle. The babies of the family are the Andean *charango* and the Mexican *requinto.* The requinto is used between verses to play fast runs and harmonies. Its high pitches soar above other guitars and percussion instruments. The *guitarrón* is the fat uncle that sings bass. It is an acoustic bass guitar usually as big as its player and hangs from a shoulder strap. The most common guitar is the *tenor* or *classic guitar.* On this instrument every variety of music can be played.

The ancestor of all these instruments is the *vihuela,* which traveled to the Americas with the Spanish and Portuguese conquerors and has since undergone many modifications. The vihuela itself had many ancestors. The idea of stretching a string over a bow attached to a soundbox probably arose during the time of the Egyptian pharaohs. Confusion exists because the origin of the word *guitar*

(top) Following his own distinctive pattern, the guitar maker begins the intricate task of assembling a rosette, the decorative circle that surrounds a guitar's soundhole. Thin slips of wood, either dyed or left their natural color, are arranged and glued together into a log, creating the desired mosaic on the end grain of the log.

(above) The mosaic logs are tapered to fit snugly together then combined with long strips of veneer around a circular form to form the rosette pattern. A year's supply of rosettes may be made at a time.

(below) Working with spruce, the wood of choice for classical guitar tops, the guitar maker planes the piece by hand, taking note of its density, texture, and directional properties.

(bottom) The rosette is carefully positioned and inserted before either the shape of the top or the soundhole is cut.

and its characteristic shape do not share a common origin. The Greek zither (cithara), Persian sitar, and Chaldean qitara have similar names but are quite unlike the family of guitars and are not considered predecessors.

Three other instruments, the kinnor, nebec, and al-oud, from Middle Eastern cultures, are similar to the guitar in the following respects. They all have a soundbox and strings that are pressed against a neck at different positions and plucked or bowed to produce different pitches. With the spread of Islamic culture and faith throughout the Middle East and North Africa, two of these instruments eventually found their way to Spain with the Moors—the al-oud and the bowed rebec. Over the centuries the al-oud evolved into the lute; the rebec began to be plucked rather than bowed and became known as the mandola. The

Lute

lute, rebec, and mandola shared the same shape, that of a half-pear. Eventually the mandola took on a new shape to become the early vihuela.

The lute, rebec, and mandola (from which the family of mandolins arises) were to remain extremely popular throughout Europe in the Middle Ages and Renaissance. The vihuela, however, was the preferred instrument in Renaissance Spain. Since it shared the same shape and attributes of the guitar, it is thought to be the guitar's true ancestor. Unlike the mandolins and lutes, which are made with a curved back and many slats of wood, the vihuela had a flat back and fewer slats. As such, it undoubtedly was a bit easier to construct. The bending of wood to make the figure-eight sides also made the vihuela easier to hold on one's thigh. Like all of the other instruments, the continued use of or-

nate rosettes surrounding the soundholes in the face expressed a Moorish heritage.

During the Renaissance the faces of the various instruments were relatively small and the reinforcement inside the top was simple lateral bracing that did not allow for much resonance. The inability of the older instruments to project sound was compensated for by using pairs of strings rather than single strings as on the modern classical guitar. These pairings were called "courses" and often the two strings were tuned an octave apart. The lute during the Renaissance had anywhere from seven or eight courses. Later, during the eighteenth century, this number of courses increased to 15 or more. The common joke of the day was that a lutenist spent half his life tuning his instrument. The reality was probably more! The vihuela initially had four courses, which eventually grew to six, so it was much easier to tune. Both instruments had frets made of catgut that were tied in place. This presented yet another bother as the frets were prone to slip out of position during play.

The vihuela was the most popular instrument of the nobility in Spain during the sixteenth century. This was the period of the conquistadors, the Spanish Golden Era. The resulting wealth of the Spanish society brought musicians from all over Spain and beyond to the courts of Valladolid and Castille. At that time the multi-voiced madrigal style of singing was much in vogue. Vihuelistas mimicked that vocal style and eventually created a distinct vihuela style of intermingling melodic lines of unsurpassed beauty.

It should be noted that along with the vihuela a sister instrument called the guitarra latina existed. This instrument was also very popular and indeed led to the development of the modern guitar. It was the same shape and approximately the same size as the vihuela but was primarily used as a strumming instrument. For that reason many of the noble vihuelistas thought the guitarra latina to be the vulgar cousin of the vihuela and disdained its use. It had four courses initially, then five, and came to be played in the same manner as the vihuela. Both of these instruments traveled across the Atlantic Ocean with the Spanish conquistadores and

Vihuelas

were important in the development of all the guitarlike instruments used in the New World.

Before we travel across the ocean from the Old World to the New World with those instruments, it should be noted that the guitarra latina would become the instrument of favor in the seventeenth and eighteenth centuries throughout Europe. This instrument was to become the five-course Baroque guitar and eventually displaced the more cumbersome lute. During the reign of Louis XIV the lute, possessing up to 30 strings, was at its zenith. There is a story that Louis XIV became fed up waiting for the lutenists to tune their instruments and hearing them continually play out of tune. He reportedly called in his music director and decreed that the lutenists be sacked in favor of Baroque guitarists!

Before we continue with the development of the guitar in Europe, we should follow the vihuela and guitarra latina to the New World. As stated before, the conquistadores and Spanish sailors brought their instruments with them. Much of the history of the guitar in the Americas parallels that of the instrument in Europe. But a strong difference existed. In Europe and Spain, in particular, the aristocratic tradition raised the classical instrument to heights at the expense of other types of guitarlike instruments. In Latin America, native influences encouraged the use of a greater variety of instruments in its abundant heritage of folk music.

The guitar, being portable and polyphonic, naturally was the instrument of choice among the explorers. Later, Christian missionaries used it to impress and convert the indigenous people. Early in the sixteenth century music schools were created in Mexico City, and the guitar and vihuela were taught alongside other

instruments. Music books of the great vihuelistas were imported and libraries were created. Indigenous music and culture was suppressed throughout Latin America and in its place Spanish and Portuguese music and instrument building were taught to further "civilize" the Indians. In Peru and Argentina, nuns and Jesuit priests encouraged the performance of European music on guitars and vihuelas by the indigenous people.

As time passed, the inevitable reassertion of native cultures resulted in the creation of different guitarlike instruments. In the Andean regions the *charango* became the preferred instrument among the native population. As is true with all folk instruments the charango is made of native-grown materials; in this case an armadillo shell serves as the body. It is a small instrument originally designed to be hidden under ponchos so that the Spanish could not detect that the Indians were creating their own music. It is strummed rather furiously and accompanies the voice or flutes in a very sweet and soulful music different from any other in the world.

In the northern parts of Latin America a variety of instruments were developed. In Venezuela the *cuatro* is used often with maracas to give the rhythm of many Venezuelan folk dances. The cuatro has a pine top that looks like an orange crate and a cedar body with four strings. The materials are generally unsophisticated and the construction is simple, but the tuning head is joined to the neck with a V joint that demands rather highly skilled crafts-

Guitarra Latina

manship. On the shoulder is a golpeador (tapguard) to protect it during powerful strumming.

In Vera Cruz, Mexico, the *jarana jarocha* is used often in conjunction with a harp and *requinto Vera Cruzano*. The jarana jarocha is also strummed rather furiously and has a

(top) The back of the guitar is made of two pieces of Indian rosewood glued together, then cut out on a bandsaw.

(above) The guitar maker taps the back and listens for its "ring" in an effort to match its sound to that of the top. The back and sides act as the sound reflector, whereas the top is the soundboard. Choice of wood used is most important. Generally, the closer the grain, the more resilient the board will be and the brighter the sound produced.

(below) The sides, also made of rosewood, are soaked in water until pliable, then shaped freehand around a hot bending iron. The shape is then checked against a template.

(bottom) The foot, neck, and head of the guitar are built out of mahogany or cedar. The design of the head is traced using a template. It and the foot will later be carved by hand.

(top left) The guitar is assembled on a workboard slightly larger than the guitar. The top is placed facedown and clamped through the soundhole. Next, the neck and sides are fitted.

(top right) The traditional pattern of fan bracing shown serves to stiffen the soundboard or top in order to achieve clear treble notes. Experimentation with bracing patterns continues.

(above) The back is fitted and glued in place. Once the glue has dried, any excess wood will be trimmed off and the edges sanded smooth.

(below) Various methods are used to hold the guitar together after gluing. Here it is wrapped with a long strip of cotton webbing in a variation of a twine-wrap method popular in South America. Other makers may use clamps or even masking tape to hold the guitar together until the glue has dried.

very elaborate golpeador. It has four double strings and is quite similar to the guitarra latina. The requinto is the traditional Mexican guitar used to play melodies in mariachi and strolling string bands. It is like a small guitar with a wider body and higher pitch. It is tuned like a guitar but at a perfect fourth interval higher. The *vihuelita* is a small five-string guitar with a sharply arched back made usually of one block of wood, which originally was probably tortoise shell. Both the vihuelita and the guitarron or bass guitar are tuned like the upper five strings of a classic guitar. The guitarron though, due to its size, is tuned an octave below a regular guitar. It is huge. A small child could fit in its body!

The *tiple* is a descendent of the guitarra latina and is played in Colombia, Venezuela, and parts of Argentina. It's impossible to say when the tiple evolved, but a report of a traveler in Argentina, José Espinosa in 1794, details a performance of the *sequidillas* (a common Spanish song) sung to the accompaniment of a tiple. In Colombia and Venezuela the tiple is used with the *bandola* to accompany a dance known as the *bambuco*, a "pursuit" dance of African origin. It has four courses of triple strings, 12 in all.

In Brazil, another small ukelele-type instrument is used to accompany the ever-popular *samba*. It is the *cavaquinho*, which has four strings and is strummed. Besides normal guitars and mandolins, the Brazilians use a seven-string guitar (with one extra bass string) to accompany a lesser-known musical form that remains popular in that country, a *choro*. The extra bass string is used to make rapid bass runs that accompany the melody instrument.

In Puerto Rico another instrument called the *Puerto Rican cuatro* is used widely by large *salsa* bands and smaller groups known as *jibaros*. It also is probably a child of the vihuela as it earlier had four courses (hence the name "cuatro"). Today, however, the cuatro is commonly made with five courses. Its distinctive construction feature is that the body is made of one piece of wood. This results in a very bright sound. It is a melody instrument played with a pick and has a heritage of being used to play such European forms as the waltz, mazurka, and polka. There are many

Caribbean forms also—*danzas, sons, aguinaldos,* and *habanera*—for which the cuatro is known.

Throughout Latin America, the most common guitar is the classic guitar. This instrument first appeared in Spain and was an extension

Jarana Jarocha

of the Baroque guitar. Its main difference was the use of six strings on a body a bit larger than the Baroque guitar. Being much easier to tune, it soon eclipsed the use of the five-course guitar.

The modern classic guitar is the culmination of centuries of acoustical research and woodcrafting techniques. The essential technique of stretching strings over a sound-box has been modified through time. The tension of the strings on the drum-head (guitar face) causes it to vibrate and create sound, which is carried to the ear. The size of the face and its ability to resonate are two of the factors that determine the sound. To withstand the tension of the strings, the back of the guitar face is braced with thin wooden strips. The pattern of bracing affects the ability of the face to vibrate. Sound travels through the bridge (the piece of wood on the face to which the strings are attached) and across the face in a concentric fashion. During the Renaissance era, instruments had comparatively small faces and were often braced in ways that did not allow much resonance. The bracing of a modern guitar is done in a fanlike fashion. This allows the face maximum freedom to vibrate and gives strength and integrity to the face. As a result modern instruments are capable of much louder, as well as richer, tones.

String technologies also had an effect on the evolution of the guitar. As was discussed previously, early instruments used double strings or courses to create more sound. The

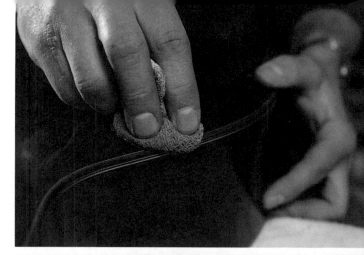

strings were made of catgut, however, and were difficult to tune. In the 1700s lutes were made with larger faces, larger and sometimes extended necks, and longer, thicker strings made from wire spun around catgut. Modern strings are made of nylon and other synthetic substances.

Guitar faces are built by cutting wood into thin slices and glueing the woods together at the edges. Using two pieces of the same wood insures that sound will travel through the wood fibers at an equal rate. The degree of thickness of the face, the hardness of the wood used, and even the thickness of the varnish applied to the face can affect a guitar's sound. Clarity of sound is further affected by the frets on the fingerboard of the neck. The practice of using catgut strings tied around the neck as frets evolved during the Renaissance into using inlaid fretwire, which improved the clarity and intonation of the instrument.

The modern classic guitar generally consists of an international collection of woods. The face is usually made of German spruce or cedar from North America. The back and sides are made of the heavier and denser rosewood, a tropical hardwood from Brazil or India. Mahogany from Central America or Spanish cedar is chosen for the neck because of its stability. African ebony is used for fingerboards because it is non-porous and smooth and wears the best. Strips of wood called "purfling" bind the seams and can be made of any number of woods. Traditional violin-type wooden pegs have been replaced by machine-made gears that tighten the strings with more control. Guitars through the ages have incorporated inlays such as tortoiseshell or ivory. The modern guitar tends to be modest with inlays in comparison to the Baroque quitar

Tiple

whose sound suffered because of the pounds of inlay used to fascinate the wealthy owners.

Musical tastes were changing in Europe. The new music of the Classical and Romantic eras, which was more single melody oriented with accompanying chords and arpeggios (chords played in a rolled or broken manner), was replacing the contrapuntal music of the Baroque era. The new guitar was more amenable to this style and soon virtuosos appeared who popularized the instrument from Spain to Russia.

To return to Latin America, it should be noted that all the advances in classical guitar development that occurred in Europe found their way to Latin America. A homegrown guitar style developed that took in the advancements of classical guitar technique and melded these with the rich heritage of South American folk music. A vast repertoire of wonderful music resulted, music that is rhythmic, peculiarly melodic, and harmonically advanced.

The classical tradition aside, it is the folk music traditions that have made the guitar in all its forms so important to Hispanic culture. This is evident throughout the Christmas season. In Mexico, for example, the nine nightly processions of *Las Posadas* feature a musical dialog that is accompanied by guitar. So too is the tradition of the *aguinaldos* in which children go from house to house singing carols and asking for gifts. In a similar tradition, Puerto Ricans travel from house to house playing guitars and cuatros and singing carols called *parrandas*. Indeed, it would be difficult to imagine Hispanic Christmas festivities without the guitar. Like the story of Jesus' nativity, the guitar has found a place deep in the hearts of the people.

(top) The finishing touches are put on a guitar. First the entire guitar, with the exception of the fingerboard, is sealed with a thin coat of shellac. Next, a filler is used, then the varnish or polish is applied. The traditional French polish is a type of shellac applied with a tightly wadded cloth pad. Used on the best guitars, it is beautiful and durable but slow and difficult to apply.

(above) After stringing, a new instrument needs to be "played in" and every note equally exercised. Otherwise, dead spots may develop.

(below) Satisfied with a job well done, guitar maker Stephen Kakos of Mound, Minnesota, relaxes in his one-man shop. He builds two instruments at a time, which take six to eight weeks to complete. Many guitars are produced in factories, but the best instruments are crafted individually in small workshops such as his.

Charango

Feliz Navidad

Five Spanish Christmas Carols

Vamos, Pastores, Vamos

E. Ciria
tr. Madeleine Forell

E. Ciria
arr. Richard Hillert

Va - mos, pas - to - res, va - mos, Va - mos a Be - lén
Come, shep - herds, come to Beth - lém, See where Je - sus lies;

A ver en e - se ni - ño La glo - ria del E - dén;
See him whose birth has saved us, Glo - ry of pa - ra - dise.

A ver en e - se ni - ño La glo - ria del E - dén
See him whose birth has saved us, The joy of pa - ra - dise.

1. E - se pre-cio-so ni - ño: Yo me mue-ro por él;
1. Beau-ti-ful ba - by Je - sus, I'd glad-ly die for him;

sus o - ji tos me en-can - tan; Su bo-qui-ta tam - bién.
His shin-ing eyes de - light me, Each per-fect lit-tle limb.

San Jo-sé lo a-ca - ri - cia; La ma-dre mi-ra en él.
Jo-seph so gent-ly strokes him; Mar-y looks on in joy;

Y los dos ex - ta - sia - dos Con - tem-plan a-quel
Caught up both in sweet rap - ture, Wor - ship their in-fant

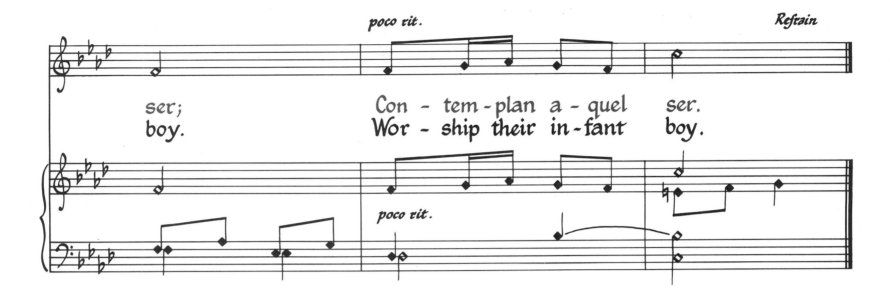

ser;
boy.
Con - tem - plan a - quel ser.
Wor - ship their in - fant boy.

2. Un establo es su cuna.
   Su casa es un portal.
   Y sobre duras pajas,
   Por nuestro amor está.
   Allí duerme el niñito,
   Junto a un mulo y a un buey;
   Y bien cobijadito,
   Con un blanco pañal;
   Con un blanco pañal. *Estribillo*

3. Es tan lindo el chiquito
   Que nunca podrá ser
   Que su belleza copien
   El lápiz y el pincel.
   Pues el eterno Padre
   Con inmenso poder
   Hizo que el Hijo fuera
   Inmenso como él;
   Inmenso como él. *Estribillo*

2. His baby bed a manger,
   His home a lowly stall,
   In straw he's humbly lying,
   With love to save us all.
   Close by his bed the animals,
   Donkey and ox, stand guard;
   Swaddled in clean white linen,
   Sleep sweetly, infant Lord.
   Sleep sweetly, infant Lord. *Refrain*

3. Such sweet and perfect beauty,
   Lovely in truth and grace,
   However great the artist,
   No human hand can trace;
   For the almighty Maker,
   God, who creates all good,
   God has begotten Jesus,
   Boundless and mighty Lord.
   Boundless and mighty Lord. *Refrain*

Ya Viene la Vieja

Traditional Spanish
tr. George K. Evans

Traditional Spanish
arr. Richard Hillert

1. Ya vie-ne la vie-ja___ Con el a-gui-nal-do___ Le pa-re-ce
1. Come, my dear old la-dy, With a lit-tle pres-ent___ That you love so

mu-cho,___ Le vie-ne qui-tan-do. Pam-pa-ni-tos ver-des, ho-jas de li-
dear-ly,___ Of-fer it to Je-sus. We're weav-ing a gar-land of green le-mon

món, La vir-gen Ma-rí-a, ma-dre del Se-ñor.
leaves, For sweet vir-gin Ma-ry, the moth-er of God.

2. Ya vienen los Reyes
Por el arenal,
Y le traen al niño
Un torre real. *Estribillo*

2. Kings of Orient riding,
Cross the sandy desert,
Bringing for the baby
Wine and cookies sweet. *Refrain*

3. Y vienen los Reyes
Por aquel camino,
Y le traen al niño
Sopitas en vino. *Estribillo*

3. Kings of Orient riding
Guided by the starlight,
Bringing to the baby
Gifts of love, this night. *Refrain*

A Adorar al Niño

Traditional Venezuelan
tr. Madeleine Forell

Traditional Venezuelan
arr. Richard Hillert

1. Aa - do - rar al ni - ño, Ven - gan los pas - to - res,
1. Come to wor - ship Je - sus, Ly - ing in the man - ger;

Aa - do - rar al ni - ño Ven - gan los pas - to - res.
Gath - er round the Christ - child, Shep - herds of each na - tion.

Que es - tá en el por - tal, Trai - gá - mos - le flo - res,
Let us bring him flowers, Sweet and love - ly tri - bute;

Que es-tá en el por - tal,   Trai - gá - mos - le flo - res.
Bless the in - fant Lord,   Joy of all cre - a - tion.

2. Una palomita
   Anunció a María,
   Una palomita
   Anunció a María
   Que en su seno santo
   El encarnaría,
   Que en su seno santo
   El encarnaría.

3. Adoro el misterio
   De la Trinidad,
   Adoro el misterio
   De la Trinidad
   Que son tres personas
   Y es un Dios, no más,
   Que son tres personas
   Y es un Dios, no más.

2. As a dove, the Spirit
   Came to visit Mary.
   Virgin mild and blessed,
   She received God's favor.
   She would bear a Son,
   Shepherd of all nations,
   From her virgin womb,
   Jesus, born our Savior.

3. Let us praise our Maker,
   Son, and Holy Spirit,
   Who has made and saved us,
   Keeps us pure and holy.
   Three in one, our God,
   Glory in the highest,
   God revealed to all
   In an infant lowly.

Cantemos con Alegría Porque Es Navidad

José Sanchez López
tr. Madeleine Forell

José Sanchez López
arr. Richard Hillert

Can - te ~ mos con a - le - grí - a Por - que es Na-vi - dad. El
Sing, Chris-tians, with mirth and glad-ness, For Christ-mas is here. Go

pue-blo de Dios ca-mi - na Con go-zo al por - tal._____
ea-ger-ly to the man-ger, God's peo-ple draw near._____

1. Dios ha ba - ja - do has - ta los, hom - bres
1. God has de - scend - ed, low - ly and earth - bound,

2. Dios no valora ciencia ni plata,
   Chico ni grande, hombre o mujer;
   Dios sólo quiere gente sencilla
   Como María, como José.
   Estribillo

2. God does not value wise words or silver,
   Small size or greatness, gender or race.
   Mary and Joseph, simple and loving,
   Such are God's people through time and space.
   Refrain

3. Jesús nos pide, desde la cuna,
   La transparencia del corazón:
   Amar a todos con alegría,
   Somos hermanos en el Señor.
   Estribillo

3. Out of the cradle, Jesus desires us
   To live in joyful, loving accord;
   Each heart transparent, open and childlike,
   Sisters and brothers, friends in the Lord.
   Refrain

En el Portal a Belén

Traditional Puerto Rican
tr. George K. Evans

Traditional Puerto Rican
arr. Richard Hillert

1. Ha na - ci - do en un por-tal___ Lle - ni - to de te - la - ra - ñas, En - tre la mu - la y el bu - ey, El Re - den - tor de las al - mas.

1. He is born with - in a sta - ble, In the bit - ter cold of win - ter; 'Twixt the ox and ass he's ly - ing, Heav-en's babe, the world's re - deem - er.

2. En el portal de Belén
   Hay estrella, sol y luna:
   La virgen y San José
   Y el niño que está en la cuna. *Estribillo*

3. Entró al portal un gallego
   Que vengo desde Galicia
   Y le traigo al niño Diós
   Lienzo para una camisa. *Estribillo*

4. Entró un gitano al portal
   De Granada vengo a aqui
   Y le traigo al niño Diós
   Un gallo quiquiriqui. *Estribillo*

2. There within the dingy stable
   Sun and moon and star are shining:
   Joseph, Mary and the baby,
   For whom all our hearts are pining. *Refrain*

3. To his side, a lowly shepherd,
   From the Spanish plains appearing,
   Brings the baby gifts of linen,
   So a shirt he can be wearing. *Refrain*

4. Also near him stands a gypsy
   From Granada he comes hieing,
   Bringing to the babe a rooster;
   "Cock-a-doodle-doo," it's crying. *Refrain*

America's First Christmas

PAUL V. D. HOYSRADT

PEOPLE TRYING TO CATCH the real spirit of Yuletide will be interested in the story of America's first Christmas. Few incidents in history provide a more promising pattern for humankind.

The chief figure in the celebration, of course, was Christopher Columbus. On Christmas Eve of the memorable year 1492 the great admiral was planning to celebrate the Feast of the Nativity with Guacanagari, who ruled over the island of Haiti. Already Columbus had received fine presents from this king. In his ignorance of West Indian geography, he believed Guacanagari to be the great Khan of Cipango, that fabulous realm of the Orient which he was sure he had found at last.

But Columbus' plans miscarried. Wearied by long watches while the *Santa Maria* cruised through the island channels, he retired to his cabin for some rest. In his absence, Juan de la Costa, the next in command, also went below to sleep; and the helmsman, seeking slumber like the others, turned over the tiller to a cabin boy.

Suddenly the flagship slid upon a coral reef. The boy felt the rudder strike and immediately gave the alarm. With Columbus in the lead, men swarmed upon the deck. Quick orders were given, a boat was lowered, but all was in vain. The *Santa Maria* was fast.

It was not long before the rolling surf, which drove the ship higher and higher upon the reef, had opened the seams. The *Santa Maria* fell over onto one side and soon the water was pouring into the hull. Columbus and the crew were forced to seek refuge on his other caravel, the *Niña*, where they passed the night.

Early the next morning the admiral sent word of the wreck to his friend Guacanagari, who promptly returned a message to Columbus, assuring him of all the assistance possible. Everything he owned was at his friend's disposal, he said. Columbus was to call for any service he needed.

Guacanagari was even better than his word. He assembled a great flotilla of canoes and sent these to the *Santa Maria* to bring all its valuables ashore. Many trips to and from the wreck were made, and everything worth saving was carried safely to the beach.

Amid all that cargo the Haitians must have seen many things that made their eyes open wide in envy. Yet so strong was their feeling of friendship for the Spaniards and so careful was Guacanagari's supervision that not a single article was stolen. Throughout the entire task of salvage their only concern seemed to be to aid the Spaniards and to bolster their spirits amid this heavy loss.

It is no wonder that Columbus was moved by such a noble spirit. In the journal that he was keeping for King Ferdinand and Queen Isabella he wrote: "These people love their neighbors as themselves; their discourse is ever sweet and gentle and accompanied by a smile. I swear to your majesties, there is not in the world a better nation or land."

After the last article had been brought ashore, Guacanagari had another plan. His guests might have missed their Christmas celebration, but there was no reason why Columbus and his crew should not enjoy the finest banquet that he and his people could provide!

It was the sort of spread that makes one's mouth water just to hear of it. There was game from the woods; lobster and fish from the sea; and all sorts of tropical fruits and vegetables. After the feasting was over and all had eaten their fill, Guacanagari led Columbus to an open grove where a thousand Haitians danced in his honor.

Columbus was deeply impressed. His host's refined manners and utmost courtesy convinced Columbus more than ever that Guacanagari was one of the earth's great noblemen.

The climax of the celebration came when the king brought out a coronet of gold, which he placed on Columbus' head, and hung plates of the same metal around his neck. There were also presents of gold for the crew. Happy at seeing his friend's delight with these gifts, Guacanagari confided that there was a gold mine not far off in the mountains where he could get as much of the metal as Columbus desired. The king's promise and limitless hospitality, not to speak of the friendliness of his subjects, led the admiral to an important decision. He resolved to found a Spanish colony on this island.

Nearly a week later Columbus gave a return banquet. By that time the Spaniards, with the help of the Haitians, had erected a fortress, and 39 of the crew made plans to stay on as the first European settlers in America. The new colony was given the name of *La Navidad*, "The Nativity," because Columbus had been saved from shipwreck on Christmas Day.

TOYS
From Dad's Workshop

BOB ARTLEY

During most of the year, my brothers and I had access to Dad's workshop where we were free to experiment in our crude attempts at making things. A few weeks before Christmas, however, this fascinating place became closed to us.

After the chores were done and supper was over Dad would put on his barn jacket and cap and disappear for the evening to his workshop. Some-times Mom would join him while we kids, burning with curiosity and excite-ment, tried to occupy ourselves as best we could until Mom returned, aglow with some Christmas secret she and Dad shared.

From our upstairs bedroom we could see the yellow light of Dad's kerosene lantern shining from the workshop window. Thus, after Mom had tucked us in for the night, we were all set for pleasant dreams.

No mansion or palace, with its many splendored trappings of the season, could have offered more of the spirit and magic of Christmas than we, as children, experienced in the frugal surroundings of our farm home. Those years, I was to learn later, were a period of financial hard times. There was barely enough money to pay for the necessities, let alone to indulge in extravagant giving that, even then, was becoming the vogue. We kids didn't know that, however. Isolated as we were on a little-used road of dirt (or mud, much of the year), our contacts were mostly with those in similar circumstances. We felt rich.

Even pouring over the magazines and mail-order catalogs that came and seeing their illustrations of well-formed and lavishly decorated Christmas trees, with attractively wrapped gifts piled high beneath, only added to our enjoyment of the season. In no way did it detract from the appreciation we felt for our own spindly tree, with its meager, mostly homemade decorations, and the modest pile of gifts beneath.

Most often these gifts were of a practical nature, clothing or books. A few inexpensive toys or games would be found too, wrapped in brightly colored or white tissue paper and placed beneath the tree or among the fragrant pine boughs. I will not forget the happy Christmas we found a wind-up train on an oval track among the wrapped packages beneath the decorated tree.

But what made Christmases so extra special for us kids were the toys that came from Dad's workshop. Along with the wonderful fragrance of evergreen boughs, the scent of freshly worked pine and new paint (barely dry) is one that will forever bring to mind those magical Christmases of my youth.

ARTLEY '88

The first toy I remember coming from Dad's workshop was a little red barn, complete with fences and cut-out wooden horses, cows, and pigs. I must have been two years old that Christmas. Dad played with me on the floor showing me how to set up the fences and put the cows in their stanchions and the horses in their stalls.

The next Christmas Dad made a wooden pull-toy dog, jointed so that it waggled when pulled. This toy was mostly for Dean who was a little over one year old at the time. As I recall, Dad made several of these toys, which were given to some of our small cousins and friends.

A little table and two chairs came from Dad's shop the Christmas I was four and Dean was two. The bright red paint was barely dry Christmas morning and permeated the house with a new-paint smell. This small-size furniture was not only fun but practical as well and was used much by my brothers and me and by our small cousins and friends when they came to visit. Down through the years, after much use, repairs, and repainting they have always remained "the little red table and chairs."

No farm is complete without a farmhouse. I must have been five the Christmas a toy house and a windmill came out of Dad's shop to join the little barn. Mom had made curtains to hang from the one window. Inside the little house was a store-bought cast-iron range. With it came an iron pot and skillet and an iron lifter that really worked for taking off the little stove lids. Also bought for the little house was a table and chair set stamped out of lithographed tin.

Under the little wooden windmill, with a wheel that turned in the wind, was a tiny iron pump. By working the little handle up and down, one could really pump water from and back into a small iron tank at its base.

In October, for his fifth birthday, Dean was given a toy locomotive made of heavy gauge metal. We both enjoyed playing with this toy, for it reflected our interest in the freight trains that daily passed through our neighborhood.

That year, as in other years, there was the pain of anticipation and the fun of trying to guess what it was that Dad was making for us for Christmas. We heard the sounds of sawing, hammering, and sanding coming from the workshop. Both our parents teased us by giving us clues as to what the big secret was. They hinted that it was black and red and about six feet long. How we puzzled over that bit of information!

Then one day, shortly before Christmas, we were stopped at a railroad crossing waiting for a string of freight cars to pass. Mom called Dad's atten-tion to a freshly painted boxcar passing before us. It was only after Christmas morning that Mom's seemingly innocent observation and Dad's acknowledgment of it had meaning for us.

The sight that greeted us that Christmas morning was one that would delight any child. Three wooden train cars, reeking of new paint and coupled to the familiar metal toy locomotive, almost dwarfed the Christmas tree and the meager supply of packages beneath. Dad had turned out a bright red boxcar, a black coal car or gondola, and a caboose, also a bright red.

We spent many gleeful moments that day, not only examining and playing with the train, but also confronting our parents concerning the ambiguous clues with which they had teased us as the train was secretly being made in Dad's shop.

Most of the toys Dad made for us were just that, toys. They were not miniature scale models of the real thing. The last toy to come out of Dad's shop for Dean and me, however, was a little haystacker that really worked, in its own small way.

As we pulled the string over two small pulleys (which Dad had made by cutting down a couple of empty spools from Mom's sewing basket) the little stacker would lift a small bunch of cut grass and deposit it in a pile that was soon a little haystack. This activity, of course, had to wait until summer.

As the years passed and Dean and I grew older, Dad no longer made gifts for us. We had graduated to things like air rifles and skiis. And, of course, books and clothes were still appreciated. But we did enjoy being in on the secrets watching the progress of the toys Dad continued to make for our younger brother and cousins.

The Christmas after Dan had turned six or seven, Dad made him a whole set of little farm buildings, including a house, barn, silo, hog house, corn crib, and machine shed. There were also some small village buildings: a church, depot, and general store. The round silo was carved from the limb of an ash tree. It had a domed roof and was painted to look like a clay block silo.

Dan and his playmates enjoyed these toys as much as Dean and I had ours. But he took better care of his and kept them for his children and now his grandchildren to enjoy.

I wish we still had the little farm buildings that Dad made for Dean and me. We would care for them as valued relics of our childhood. But, sad to say, the little house, barn, and windmill, much like their full-scale counterparts across the country, have disintegrated back into the earth from which they came. These toys, as well as others Dad made for us, have become a part of the soil beneath the shade of the maples where we so often played with them.

I suppose it is only in the maturity of our latter years that we value the artifacts of our lives as objects of historical value or treasured keepsakes. In hindsight I cannot imagine why we didn't take better care of those heirlooms, which they certainly were. But as children we did value them highly as toys to use and to enjoy for that brief moment of childhood.

ARTLEY '88

Season of Joy
in Mexico

JAMES PETERSON

IT IS MID-DECEMBER. In the small, dark room
that one man calls home one corner has taken on a
special character. A worn but still beautiful blanket
covers several cardboard boxes that have been
grouped together. The boxes' varying sizes create an il-
lusion in the subdued light of a location in the countryside, one that could represent this man's place of origin.
Placed on the blanket with obvious care and in appropriate relation to one another are tiny figures, almost one
hundred of them, representing the holy family, the three
kings, the shepherds and their goats, and many other
people of varying shapes and sizes.

Clearly, once more it's *Navidad*!

It is mid-December. In twos and threes they come.
They live here in this small town about an hour's drive
from that urban sprawl known as Mexico City. Each night
during this time of the year they gather in the quaint
village chapel for the novena.

---

*(above) Hundreds of pilgrims join in colorful procession on
their way to the Basilica of Guadalupe on December 12.*

The elements needed for the service—flowers by the
armful, candles, musical instruments, mimeographed
song sheets (not used this night for the first time judging
by their condition)—gradually are assembled as brought
by various people.

Soon the chapel is filled with children, many of them,
young men and women, older people, and even dogs.
As the people gather, *abrazos* (embraces) are exchanged
accompanied by warm smiles and cheerful words of
greeting interspersed over and over again with "*¡Feliz
Navidad!*"

Clearly, once more it's Christmas!

In mansions regal in appearance and in dwellings fash-
ioned from cardboard and shielded by remnants of plas-
tic, in humble wayside chapels and in the stately cathe-
drals, in the rural countryside and in the urban sprawl
of Mexico's cities each year the profound mystery of
Christmas comes alive.

December has arrived. And in Mexico, as in much of
the rest of the world, preparations have begun for the
celebrations of the Christmas season. In every country,

in every culture, the festivities take different forms. In Mexico they have acquired characteristics that do not exist anywhere else.

From the first minute of December 12, the Day of the Virgin of Guadalupe, to the last minute of January 6, Three Kings Day, celebration and a sense of something special permeate the land. In the countryside, in remote villages, and in the crowded urban areas, *Navidad* is a time for celebration, a time for color and pageantry, a time for music and dancing. It is a time of respite in the daily struggle to survive.

The Day of the Virgin of Guadalupe

On December 12, Mexico celebrates what is perhaps its most important religious holiday, the Day of the Virgin of Guadalupe. The Virgin is variously called the Empress, Patroness, and Protectress of the Americas. Hundreds of thousands of men, women, and children annually pilgrimage to the Basilica of Guadalupe to express their reverence and respect for her.

During the several days preceding the festival, vehicles of all types fill the streets of Mexico City, bringing pilgrims for the day. Many others walk for miles to attend. Dancing and music and song fill the air. Truly a religious fiesta, the day offers several high masses in which the pilgrims may take part.

To understand why this day exerts such an influence on the Mexican populace, one must know the legend behind the day. The Virgin of Guadalupe, the devout believe, was the appearance of the same spirit who, while incarnate as a woman named Mary 2000 years ago, conceived and gave birth to Jesus Christ. The Virgin of Guadalupe is also thought to have been the same spirit who appeared to Bernadette at Lourdes and to three children at Fatima more recently. The devout consider Mexico a highly privileged country because of her appearance there. The sight of almost a quarter of a million believers gathered at the Basilica on December 12 is not only inspiring, but it is also a mere token of the great faith in the legend the people of Mexico have. The legend

has spiritually galvanized the nation and sustains and comforts millions.

The simple story of Juan Diego, a peasant farmer, regarding his vision of the Virgin and his humble transmission of her message to the Bishop initiated all that has become a part of this tradition. Her message was that she desired that a temple be built on the site of her encounter with Diego where, as she said, "I can show and offer all my love, compassion, help, and protection."

Whether, as skeptics suggest, this legend was propagated by church authorities to establish Christianity more quickly following the conquest by Spain or, as devoted millions have believed, that this is the account of a miracle, there is little doubt that the legend has been a powerful force in the lives of many over the centuries.

An Order of Religious Sisters has made this legend and the tradition that has developed over time a matter of research, seeking to understand the influence and power it continues to exert. As the sisters share the results of their labors with visitors, their manner is reminiscent of the simple peasant, Juan Diego. They speak of the legend as a power for liberation in the lives of those who have known from personal experience the varied expressions of oppression. And in manner shy and understated they suggest to listeners that, perhaps, sometimes *El Señor* (the Lord), sees it necessary to bypass the institutional church and to use the little ones, the lowly, to show God's presence among them, to show the love, compassion, help, and protection that the Creator, Redeemer, and Sustainer offers to everyone.

Las Posadas

It might be noted that a number of Christmas customs in Mexico are properly designated as national in character. Many consider *Las Posadas* (the Inns, also called the "Journeys" or "Nine Nights") to be one of the most important of these traditions.

During the nine nights preceding *Navidad* (Christmas Day) entire communities, neighborhoods, or local streets join in a series of nine processions reenacting Mary's and

(left) The Three Kings are honored on January 6, the traditional day of gift-giving. Children put their shoes out the night before to be filled by the visiting Magi. (center) The most important religious holiday in Mexico, the Day of the Virgin of Guadalupe draws hundreds of thousands of worshipers to the Basilica. (right) Christmas decoration in the Zocalo.

Joseph's search for lodging in Bethlehem. The number nine recalls both the Roman Catholic tradition of novena or nine days' devotion and the nine months of Mary's pregnancy.

The continuum of society, ranging from extreme affluence to extreme poverty, is reflected in the manner of celebrating *Las Posadas*. The affluent celebrate with extravagant costumes and overflowing tables of food in contrast to the less fortunate who celebrate with simple clothing and a door-to-door processional followed by punch and cookies.

In her well-known letters on life in Mexico one hundred years ago, the Marchioness Calderon de la Barca described *Las Posadas* as experienced in the mid-1800s:

"This is the last night of the so-called *Posadas*; a curious mixture of devotion and fun, but in a very touching setting. . . . The holy family's journey is represented throughout nine days, and it seems more as if it's done for the children than for serious purposes. . . . An army of children, dressed as angels, was joined to the procession. Their clothing was of white feathers, a profusion of fine diamonds and pearls in bandeaux, brooches and necklaces, white gauze wings, and white satin shoes with gold edges; young people dressed as shepherds and a magnificent nativity scene. We returned to the living room—angels, shepherds and other guests—and there was dancing until we dined."

As it was in the 1800s, so it remains today, with appropriate updating. While such a description applies only to a small percentage of the populations, it is true that a family of any economic category might well spend, literally, everything it possesses in order to host at least one of the nine *Posada* parties.

In a typical Mexican neighborhood, the families who live on a block may begin weeks in advance preparing for these special days. Each family takes a part.

The day of the first *Posada*, the street is closed off at either end of the block. The sidewalks and the street itself are swept. Pastel colored paper displaying a variety of cut-out patterns is strung on lines criss-crossing the street from one end to the other. Children with evident excitement run up and down the street, laughing and teasing and shouting to each other.

As the appointed hour draws near, the children are summoned to their homes. It is time to get dressed. Other family members set up tables that will hold the refreshments. Still others climb to the rooftop where the *piñata* is hung. A rope is attached to the *piñata* so that it can be managed by the young men later in the evening.

Decorations made of straw and adorned with brightly colored ribbons are attached to the doorposts of each home where they silently add to the festive atmosphere.

Gradually the people assemble in the street. Boys and girls, dressed in their very best, talk with one another a bit more hesitantly now, perhaps a little uncomfortable in their special attire.

Soon it is apparent that something is happening at the end of the street. Children, forgetting their finery, run and gather where a burro, rented for the evening, appears looking a bit uncertain about its coming role.

As the moment for the procession approaches, children from the host families appear dressed as members of the holy family, the three kings, and the shepherds.

A man chosen as the leader for the evening assembles the families. The candles are lighted, copies of the songs are distributed, and finally the procession begins.

Everyone joins in singing the traditional songs as the procession moves down the street, stopping at each door. At each stop, several people leave the assembly to enquire at the house if there is room.

Ultimately, at the house chosen for that evening's entertainment, everyone is welcomed. Yes, there is room here. Crowding onto the modest patio, everyone gazes with admiration at the host family's *nacimiento* (manger scene), which is arranged with care just outside the front door.

In twos and threes the neighbors move to the refreshment tables. Tamales, *dulces* (sweets), beautifully decorated cookies, and punch accompany animated conversation and laughter.

Little Lights of Christmas

PHYLLIS W. HEALD

ENCHANTING IS THE WORD for luminarias, those "little lights" traditional to Mexico and the Southwest at Christmastime. Simple, effective decorations, these rows of candles in their brown paper bags turn houses into fairy castles and gardens into heavenly vistas.

Actually, luminarias are as old as Christianity itself. The original "little lights" traditionally were bonfires built by shepherds to guide the holy family toward Bethlehem. For centuries after, small bonfires continued to be used on Christmas Eve. Made of pitchwood and spaced a few feet apart in double rows, they formed a path always leading to the entrance of a dwelling, symbolically lighting the way for the *Niño*.

As time went on and living became more gracious in the western world, people began to substitute candles for the bonfires. Placed in beds of sand and protected from the elements by scraps of paper, the candles burned all through the night of Christmas Eve.

Oddly enough it was Yankee traders who brought the final change to luminarias. About 150 years ago traders arrived in the Southwest with paper sacks. No one was more surprised than they when they found their wares—brown, plain and uninspired—sought avidly by the local people. The ingenious *señoras* would fill each bag one-third with sand, fold its top edge down to form a cuff, then nestle a candle deep inside. Sturdy, safe, and shining with the bewitching glow of a subdued spotlight, luminarias took on an added glory.

Today they are made in exactly the same way, except for the candle. Now, special luminaria candles are cast by the tens of thousands. Shaped for practicability, not for tapered beauty, they are short, thick, solid, and designed to burn for 15 hours.

Luminarias were converted quite by accident from a simple religious expression into decoration. According to the story, a great party was planned on

Later the children delight in the energetic ritual of breaking the *piñata*, a colorful figure made of papier mâché and filled with treats and trinkets. Each child is blindfolded and handed a stick with which to strike the *piñata*. The fun is prolonged by the operator of the rope who raises or lowers the *piñata*, making it more difficult to hit. Finally, one of the children strikes home, scattering the contents of the *piñata* on the floor, and everyone scrambles to get their share of the loot.

Christmas Eve and Christmas Day itself for many center in the home and the parish church. On Christmas Eve families and friends gather to await the birth of the Christ child. Depending on economic circumstances, the meal that is served may be either a splendid feast or a simple repast. In any case, the meal is made festive by the color and cheer of flowers (especially the poinsettia), bells, and lights. At the appropriate hour, the people crowd into the parish churches for the midnight mass. The service ranges in style from the highly formal ritual of the cathedral to the almost casual celebration of the base ecclesial communities. In either place, music and singing are central features of the worship, accompanied by the powerful tones of a mighty organ or by the inviting chords of simple guitars.

In the mixture of the rituals of celebration and in the ordinary conversation and sharing that takes place, the bonds between neighbors and families are strengthened.

Three Kings Day

Three Kings Day, January 6, has been and for many still is a moment of beauty and love in a season of beauty and love. Rooted in the biblical account of gifts brought by the Magi to the infant Jesus, the traditions of Three Kings Day have evolved. The custom of gift giving, especially to the children, has a long history, dating way back to the 16th century. Spanish missionaries used nativity scenes and masses as means of teaching Christianity to the Indians. The custom of giving presents emerged as each night, after the religious ceremony, the Christ child was praised in song, prayers were offered, and sweets were passed out.

Anchoring the end of the Christmas season, Three Kings Day abounds in customs. On the night of January 5 children set out their shoes to await a visit from the Three Kings before going off to bed. The shoes are put in an accessible place for the Magi, along with a gift for the camels (bundles of hay or freshly cut grasses). Early the next morning brings expectant young ones eager to see if gifts have been left for them.

For many of the more affluent, the emergence of Santa Claus has replaced much of the wonder of Three Kings Day. Yet for most this day continues its particular importance.

It has often been recognized that the essence of celebration is a part of the reality known perhaps best by the very poor. And in Mexico many millions know that condition. While it may be true that the religious sentiment has survived in small nuclei only, the December customs have come to be the cultural patrimony of all Mexicans. Institutions such as Secretariat of Public Education and the National Fund for Promoting Craftsmanship sponsor various events in places like the National Auditorium of Popular Cultures and others with the purpose of saving Mexican traditions and promoting greater interaction among the people. These events include such different offerings as plays, traditional foods, nativity scenes, piñatas, posadas, stories, Christmas paintings, toys, and photographs.

Perhaps few countries around the world manage to experience the season of *Navidad* as joyously and as energetically as does Mexico. The plazas, the streets, the houses are gathering places. Young and old, families, neighbors, and strangers are caught up in that "something special" that is almost tangible.

The *Navidad* of Mexico is not just one day or several days; it is a composite of days. It is indeed a season. And it is a time when perhaps one of this nation's principle natural resources shines forth most clearly. That resource is joyousness or gaity, which expresses itself in bold colors and glitter and brightness—all in a kind of spontaneous rejoicing that everyone can enjoy.

Christmas at the Palace of the Territorial Governor of New Mexico. Nobody could think of an appropriate way to decorate the building. Finally, someone had the inspiration of using luminarias to light the house and grounds. Hundreds of candles in brown paper bags were spotted along the roof, on window sills, outlining paths, and through the extensive gardens. The result was sheer magic.

Years later, when a fraternity of the University of New Mexico was too low in funds to buy decorations for its house, one of the men remembered the story of the Governor's Palace. Sacks and candles were cheap. Sand was free. So luminarias were used profusely and again with such striking effect that the entire university took over the idea. Now, each Christmas, its many buildings glow with more than 8000 "little lights."

As Mexico opened to North American enterprise and trade, a tremendous influx of different holiday traditions came to the Southwest. Santa Claus, Christmas trees, and reindeer bells replaced *Las Posadas* processions, *piñata* parties, and luminaria displays. But now the pendulum swings and Southwesterners are turning again to their rich, distinctive heritage. The old customs stand side-by-side with the new. It is not unusual to see a jolly Saint Nick and his reindeer next door to a gentle manger scene illuminated by the soft flickering luminarias.

In churches it is not unusual to see luminarias displayed in clusters. Often the candles are set in tall translucent glasses, sometimes colored red or yellow, and placed on altars, at windows, in niches, or beneath religious paintings. These small luminaria arrangements appear in groups of twelve, nine, or seven to symbolize the twelve apostles, the nine principals of the nativity, or simply Mary, Joseph, Jesus, a lamb, and the three Magi.

And so, each year on Christmas Eve, in towns along the border, in cities and on ranches, one sees more and more of the glowing "little lights." As the number of luminarias increases, so may the hope of everlasting peace, for these decorations of the nativity were truly meant to light the way for Christ.

50

Adoration of the Shepherds

El Greco (Domenikos Theotocopoulos) 1541-1614

PHILLIP GUGEL

SOMETIME BETWEEN 1612 and 1614 El Greco painted his fifth and last version of the shepherds' visit to the Christ child, a favorite subject of his. The painting, an altarpiece, graced his tomb-chapel, the convent church of Santo Domingo el Antiguo in Toledo, Spain, for over 300 years. His body was removed from the church during a dispute in 1619. The painting, however, remained there until 1954 when it was sold to the Prado Museum in Madrid.

Born on the Greek island of Crete, El Greco (which means "The Greek") spent his artistic career in Toledo, where he enjoyed the patronage of the church, participated in the city's cultural life, was friends with distinguished intellectuals and clergy, and lived extravagantly off his large income for 37 years.

What is striking about the *Adoration* is its distorted and unrealistic style, resulting from El Greco's unusual treatment of color, form, light, and space to express the awe and ecstasy he felt over the revelation of God's Son.

Neoplatonist philosophy influenced El Greco's treatment of light. Central to Neoplatonism was the view that the physical world was inferior to the spiritual realm. According to an inventory of the artist's library, El Greco owned a copy of Pseudo-Dionysius' *Celestial Hierarchy*, which used a complex philosophy of light to explain God, from whom we receive divine illumination. Reflecting such ideas, El Greco's light shines from the infant's oddly proportioned body and symbolizes God's light.

Jesus appears fearful as he reaches for Mary, as though startled by the ox's nearness or the ecstatic visitors. As the bringer of divine light, he emits a radiance that creates dramatic contrasts of light and shadow on the figures and surrounding space. This radiance defines their contours and makes the rich colors of their apparel even richer.

Though clad in her customary blue and red garb, Mary neither kneels nor reclines in adoration as is common in medieval nativity scenes. She stands and removes her son's swaddling cloths, a tranquil gesture that signifies Jesus' revelation to those present, as well as to all humankind.

Joseph's expressive facial profile and hands, expansive gesture, elongated anatomy, and contorted, unbalanced stance reveal his feelings of wonderment. The child's radiance imparts a shadowy, glowing richness to the yellow and blue-gray hues of Joseph's heavy clothing. These distortions of color, form, and light transform Joseph into an ecstatic spiritual figure, quite unlike the passive earthly guardian so often depicted.

As was customary, El Greco's trio of shepherds includes an elderly, a middle-aged, and a young peasant type. Beyond that, his innovative portrayal gives them a majesty out of proportion to their humble station in life. One scholar suggests that El Greco painted himself as the elderly shepherd in the foreground, whose elongated body seems lofty even though he kneels. There is a wonderful play of light and shadow on his legs, making them look three-dimensional. Defined through loose brushwork, the figure rests at an angle so that the light striking it causes the left edges of his orange jerkin and yellow breeches to glow like embers against his shadowy back. The elderly shepherd's aristocratic nose and goatee accent his sensitively rendered profile as he adores the child.

Opposite him the middle-aged shepherd, whose green jerkin becomes partially yellow in the light, seems lost in contemplation as he gazes down, his arms raised in devotion. The young shepherd, towering between them with arms crossed in adoration, appears the most mystical of the three. Light playing on his knobby limbs makes their elongation more pronounced and imparts an incandescence to his yellow jerkin and blue breaches. The halo of clouds highlights his profile and unites him with the angelic realm above.

El Greco's unusual treatments of color, form, light, and space express his awe and ecstasy over God's Son.

Placed at different heights around the Christ child, his parents and the shepherds form a compact oval group surrounding him. Almost hidden within this group, the reclining ox raises its horned head between Joseph and the elderly shepherd, a surprising innovation!

A bound lamb beneath the young shepherd's right foot recalls John the Baptist's heralding of Jesus as the Lamb of God. Behind his left thigh a donkey's shadowy head merges with the darkness.

Overhead, the closeness of the hovering angels and cherubs to the figures below effectively erases the boundary between heaven and earth, as does the vertical dimension of the canvas and the cloudy indistinct background with its dark edges. These features serve to distort the scene's space, making it ambiguous.

The angel on the left holds aloft a banderole inscribed with the Latin phrases for "Glory in the highest" and "On earth peace," while his female counterpart hovers in adoration opposite him. Between them an apparition looks down; scholars are silent about this peculiar detail. The fluttering cherubs, who exhibit such exuberant contortions as they gaze in wonder, are simply a visual delight.

Crowded with figures, the *Adoration* imparts spiritual significance to the shepherds' visit at Jesus' birth. Drawing from his own religious vision, El Greco invites the viewer also to approach the manger and so enter heaven's bright courts.

The Black Madonna

JEAN LOUISE SMITH

Few travelers who go to Barcelona, Spain, fail to take a day to journey to Montserrat to see the Black Madonna, for this ancient carved wooden figure of Mary and her child is mysterious in origin and surrounded with legend. It inspired Richard Wagner to write his famed opera, *Parsifal,* and both Goethe and Schiller to write poetry.

The oldest legend about the Black Madonna is that the apostle Luke carved the figure and that it was brought to Spain by Peter during those early years when Christianity was taken to the far reaches of the Mediterranean world. Another old story claims that shepherds found the carved figure in the year 880, hidden in Cueva Cave, where it may have been sheltered during the Moorish occupation of Spain. There are even those who believe that the carving is so beautiful that it must have been done by other than human hands.

Whatever its early history, the Black Madonna has since the twelfth century been kept in the Benedictine monastery of Montserrat. Its uniqueness comes from its being carved from a single piece of wood, beautifully painted rich tones of gold, with the faces of Mary and the child unmistakably black. These dark features were not intentional, but rather are the result of the natural aging of the wood combined with the smoke of constantly burning candles over the centuries.

Most visitors first see the Black Madonna from the far end of the basilica, where it is in a niche high above the altar. Even from this distance, the figure is impressive and moving. As one comes closer, details come into focus: Mary is seated on a low throne, her expression is sad and thoughtful. Her bearing is truly regal, but at the same time warm and maternal. The child whom she holds on her knees is crowned and dressed like a king, as he was traditionally shown in medieval

The Black Madonna, one of the ancient treasures of Christendom, is visited in Barcelona, Spain, by thousands of worshipers each year. This elegant masterpiece is surrounded by an aura of mystery, for its origins are unknown.

art. His right hand is raised in blessing and in the left he holds a bursting pomegranate, Christ's special symbol of royalty and of resurrection. Mary extends a globe of the world in her right hand, to represent the worldwide message of the gospel.

Most modern pilgrims arrive at Montserrat by bus or car, usually by way of the 32 miles northwest from Barcelona. Most of the trip is on a plain, but suddenly the "serrated mountain" appears (from which the name Montserrat is derived), rising to 2380 feet from the plain. It is a startling view, for the masses of stone are weirdly and strangely shaped into pillars and humps caused by erosion long centuries ago. The climb up the mountain is very steep, and the crowds are unbelievably great once the monastery is reached, but the journey is worth the effort on seeing the strangely beautiful and mysterious Black Madonna.

Scarcely a whisper is heard among the throngs who slowly mount the steps to the alcove high above the altar to see Mary and her child. The reverent atmosphere is intensified by the light of flickering candles, the scent of greens adorning the chapel, the sound of worshipers praying both familiar and special seasonal prayers, and the beautiful strains of "Salve Regina," which is sung each day by a boys choir. In addition to the beautiful church, there is a museum where visitors can learn about work that the monks at Montserrat carry on today.

Kings have made pilgrimages to the mount, and common people have gone there in countless numbers. So loved is this spot that many a Catalonian girl has been named Montserrat. The arts of Christendom have produced countless representations of the madonna and child, but this ancient and beautiful figure of the Black Madonna creates a reverence for many above all others.

Mother Merryweather's Plum Pudding

LOUISE CARROLL

POLLY'S VOICE was full of longing, "We always had plum pudding. Roast goose, brussel sprouts, and plum pudding."

Impatiently Arletta tossed her head, "Honestly, Polly, I'm tired of hearing about plum pudding."

"Well, I just mentioned that we had plum pudding."

Arletta muttered to herself, "Plum pudding. Polly plum pudding." Louder she said, "I've decided against spending Christmas with my son. He and Debbie just fuss over me too much. I would rather spend the day quietly. Of course, they're begging me to come. I just had another letter from them."

Earlier that morning Arletta had carefully shredded the letter into little pieces before she dropped it into the garbage on top of a gutted grapefruit half. It had read:

> *Dear Mom,*
>
> *Debbie and I are going to spend Christmas on a skiing vacation. We have been looking forward to it for a long time. Perhaps we'll see you in the Spring. Enclosed is a check for you. Have a Merry Christmas.*
>
> > *With love,*
> > *Dirk*

Suddenly remembering her friends, Arletta continued, "I really don't like all that fussing. A good bowl of soup and a quiet day suit me better."

Polly nodded, "There's nothing like a good bowl of soup. I wouldn't mind that, but at home we always had plum pudding."

"Oh, Polly!" Arletta groaned at the mention of plum pudding again.

That Polly is a good old soul, but I get tired of hearing about her old Christmas meals and plum pudding.

Polly looked down at her well-worn shoes but didn't really see them. Christmas was just a week away and she didn't want to think about another lonely holiday. Of course, she could go to the Mission. They had nice Christmas dinners there with all the trimmings and it was free. But the thought of all those lonely people there each shut up in their own compartment of loneliness depressed her. It was easier for Polly to be lonely at home. But homemade soup at a table with friends would be good. Of course, Arletta never made real homemade soup. Her idea of soup was the kind from a can. Polly had hoped that Arletta would invite her, but now Arletta was irritated at her over the plum pudding. Polly was sorry she had mentioned the plum pudding again, but it had been on her mind.

Here in the large, cheerful, social room at the Senior Citizens Center, Arletta, Polly, and Fanny met often. As usual Fanny Merryweather was content to sit quietly and listen to Arletta and Polly. This day, however, Fanny surprised them by speaking loudly, "I'm going to my niece's for Christmas dinner."

The other two turned to her to hear more, but Fanny just smiled and nodded.

Using her cane to help her, Polly leaned forward, "Well, I'll be going now. If I don't see you two before, you have a merry Christmas."

"Merry Christmas, Polly," Fanny said softly and smiled.

As Polly began to walk away Arletta called after her, "Where are you going for Christmas?"

Immediately Arletta was sorry. She knew Polly didn't have anyone or anywhere to go. Well, neither do I, Arletta thought. Before Polly could answer Arletta went on, "I was hoping if you hadn't made any plans you might have Christmas dinner with me."

Polly's face, with all its rather dusty looking wrinkles, arranged itself quickly into a happy look. She smiled broadly, "Yes, I would really like that."

Arletta was relieved Polly had accepted, but she kept her voice casual, "You know I'm not much of a cook. We'll have some soup."

"Oh, that will be fine. I always like soup. I'll see you then."

As Polly walked away Arletta turned to Fanny, "That Polly is a good old soul, but I get tired of hearing about her old Christmas meals and plum pudding. Every Christmas she starts on that plum pudding."

"I have my mother's recipe for plum pudding," Fanny volunteered. Arletta waited for Fanny to elaborate, but Fanny just nodded and smiled.

The next day the thought came to Arletta to have something special for Christmas dinner. What did Polly say they always had? Roast goose. Immediately Arletta dismissed that idea. Brussel sprouts. "Oh, no," thought Arletta, "I will not have them for Christmas. I never liked them."

Plum pudding. Of course! Having never eaten plum pudding, she could come up with only a vague idea of what it was.

Later in the evening Arletta thought again of plum pudding. Not being one to care much about cooking, she didn't have any cookbooks. She took a quick look at some holiday recipes in a recent magazine but didn't find any for pudding, plum or otherwise.

Early the next morning Arletta walked the three blocks to Fanny Merryweather's apartment. Laboriously she copied Mother Merryweather's plum pudding recipe

from a yellowed piece of tablet paper that Fanny found after a long search through a cardboard box of miscellaneous old papers. Arletta smiled to herself as she copied the last line of the recipe: "Make one for a friend." She thought how happy Polly would be.

Back at her own apartment Arletta sat down for her morning tea. She unfolded the recipe and began to make a list of the ingredients she would need to buy. As she wrote ¼ pound suet, she sighed. Arletta wasn't even certain what suet was. Something to do with meat it seemed, probably fat. Ugh. Brown sugar. She didn't even have any white sugar. In the ongoing battle of losing weight Arletta used artificial sweeteners. Raisins. Currants. Currants? As she listed the peels and citrons she shook her head impatiently. Who ever heard of these things? Who ever heard of eating them? Plain old food was what she ate. Arletta congratulated herself that she had never gotten interested in cooking.

With an air of finality Arletta closed the cupboard door. Polly could eat soup—like it or lump it.

The next day at the supermarket, Arletta lingered at the meat counter. Although there were many selections, well wrapped and well displayed, she could not find suet.

With a definite feeling of irritation Arletta rang the bell for service. Immediately a pleasant young woman in a white coat appeared. "Can I help you?" She asked.

"Yes, I would like a quarter pound of saw-ette."

"A quarter pound of what?"

"Sweat."

"Sweat?"

Arletta changed the pronunciation again, "Sut."

"Sut?"

As the young woman's face remained blank, Arletta, her voice rising, tried again, "Soot."

"Soot? I'm sorry, I'm not sure what you need. What do you plan to do with it? Maybe we have something else."

Hearing the loud voices, an older man in a white coat and hat had come from the cutting room behind the counter to help. His voice was strong and good-natured, "She's making Christmas plum pudding," he said with assurance.

Gratefully Arletta smiled, "How did you know?"

"Well, this time of year I thought it might be. We always have plum pudding for Christmas."

"You and Polly."

"Polly? I beg your pardon?"

"Just a friend of mine. She likes plum pudding, too."

Soon he returned with a small, white-wrapped package, "Next time you have a problem, just ask for me, Bill Reamly."

"Thank you for helping me. I'm Arletta Blackmere."

By the next day the glow from shopping faded and Arletta began to feel foolish. "Why you silly old plum pudding! To think you were going to spend Christmas Day doing the one thing you have avoided better than anyone most of your life. Just because silly old holly Polly plum pudding is coming to dinner you get a pudding notion to cook something as complicated as that. Look at this bunch of uneatable junk sitting around. Flour . . . peels . . . yuck!

Being a tall woman with long arms Arletta had no trouble putting the ingredients up in the top shelf of her cupboard. With an air of finality she closed the cupboard door. Polly could eat soup—like it or lump it. And with that she went to bed.

Arletta slept well and was up early the next day. The endless morning was followed by a long afternoon and an even longer evening. Arletta was tempted to go to the store again, but told herself this running to the store every day was a silly habit that had to stop.

The next day Arletta woke with a headache and spent the morning lying in bed. Finally in the afternoon she went down to the lobby that doubled as a social room. Mr. and Mrs. Hampton were sitting there. They looked alike; white hair, white skin, same size, same clear blue eyes. They greeted her with identical smiles, "Mrs. Blackmere, nice to see you."

"Nice to see you, too. Seems everyone is busy with the holidays," Arletta commented as she looked around the empty room.

"Yes, indeed. We're waiting here for our daughter. We're going to stay with her until after New Year's."

"How nice for you," Arletta replied. "My son, Dirk, begged me to come to his place, but you know how children fuss so, and I just can't take all that bothering over me. Gives me a headache."

The Hamptons both agreed. Not wanting to meet the loving daughter who was coming to take her parents away for the holidays, Arletta made an excuse and hurried back to her apartment. She fixed tea and toast and went to bed.

After a restless night Arletta woke in the morning feeling dull and listless. As she fixed her cereal she found the milk had turned sour. Arletta ate toast and tea as she listened to the radio. Abruptly she turned the radio off

and addressed it with feeling, "You and I know Christmas doesn't make anyone happy. It only makes people realize how miserable they are. Sing all the happy tunes you want, I'm not listening!"

Although it was a cold, gray day Arletta could not put off going shopping any longer. She needed more milk and she was low on tea bags. Quickly she walked the few blocks to the store, thinking formless, sad thoughts along the way. At one point she had to take deep breaths to keep from crying. At the store shoppers were hurrying about pushing the carts in front of them as protection from the other carts coming toward them. Their faces looked tense and they did not appear to hear the message in the Christmas music being played in the background.

A good-natured voice behind her stopped her unhappy thoughts, "Mrs. Blackmere. Is that you?"

Turning, Arletta looked into the smiling eyes of Bill Reamly. "It's me," she replied.

As they stood and talked over a cup of coffee at the coffee machine Arletta's mood brightened.

Walking home Arletta felt better. She was impressed with the attention Bill had given her. She felt younger and hummed Christmas music as she walked. Maybe this going to the store wasn't such a bad idea after all. Suddenly she remembered her headache and was grateful it was gone.

On Christmas Eve Arletta made one more trip to the store for the next day's dinner. She bought a big package of frozen fried chicken, a can of sweet potatoes, and a can of cranberry sauce. Thinking of what a nice meal she would be fixing for Polly, she also bought a package of paper napkins with red and silver bells in the corner.

Christmas only makes people realize how miserable they are.

Arletta was smiling as she slowly passed the meat counter and stopped when Bill Reamly spoke, "Why, Arletta, you look absolutely glowing. Makes me happy just to see you smile."

Arletta's laugh rang through the corridor.

Bill laughed too, "Now you have a merry Christmas, and don't eat too much of that plum pudding."

Arletta smiled again and waved, but somehow the mention of the plum pudding made her feel as though she had lost something, something precious.

On Christmas Day Arletta woke far too early. It was gray and cold outside. The sky looks like plum pudding, she thought. She smiled to herself, "You silly old Christmas goose. You don't even know what plum pudding looks like!"

As she prepared her breakfast tea, the words echoed in her mind, plum pudding, plum pudding. Why call it plum pudding? Were there plums in it? Being curious she unfolded the recipe and read it again. There were no plums in it. Studying it more closely, she thought it didn't really look too difficult after all; besides she had the ingredients.

Plunging ahead before she could change her mind, Arletta began to mix the ingredients, carefully following each step of the recipe. Abruptly she stopped—¼ teaspoon nutmeg and ¼ teaspoon of mace. She knew without looking that she didn't have either. "Now look at the mess you got yourself into," Arletta scolded herself.

Thinking she could borrow the needed spices, Arletta went to the Hamptons' on the next floor and rang the doorbell before she remembered they had gone to their daughter's for the holidays. Since the store wasn't open she stood in the hall, uncertain of what to do. Looking around she recalled George Fierro who lived next door to the Hamptons. Without stopping to think that she knew him only slightly, Arletta knocked on his door. At the second knock George opened the door. Arletta was cheerful. "Merry Christmas, George," she said.

George was hard of hearing, his eyesight was failing, and he had only met Arletta once before, so he found it difficult to recognize her.

Arletta forged ahead, "George, do you have some mace?"

"Mace? What happened? You got a burglar?"

"No, not that kind of mace, the kind you use in baking," Arletta answered. "It's a spice, I think. I'm making plum pudding and I don't have any mace or nutmeg."

"Plum pudding? Never heard of it. But eggs, yes, I got eggs."

"No, not eggs, George," Arletta corrected, "nutmeg. Nutmeg and mace."

"Nutmeg and mace, huh? I don't cook much. I don't think I have those things."

Shoulders sagging, Arletta began to walk away. "Have a merry Christmas, George," she managed to say.

As she walked away, George tried to recall her name. Finally to stop her, he called, "Mrs. Mrs."

"Yes?" Arletta turned around.

"Come in and look in the kitchen. There's some things left from when my wife cooked."

Inside the neat apartment Arletta easily found the mace and nutmeg in a box of spices in the cupboard. George's apartment, so identical to her own, made her think perhaps they shared the same problem. On an impulse she invited George to dinner. She wrote her apartment number on a piece of note paper and urged him to come for Christmas dinner with her and Polly.

Why call it plum pudding? Were there any plums in it? She unfolded the recipe and read it again.

Back in her apartment a happy-hearted Arletta added the spices and finished the mixing. The next direction read, "Turn into a greased, tightly closed pudding mold." Arletta almost jumped. Pudding mold? Aloud she said, "What in the great blue blazes is a pudding mold?"

Dumbly she stared at the recipe and then at the bowl of raw, gooey plum pudding. For a full ten seconds Arletta fought the impulse to throw it all in the garbage can. But instead she resolutely put on her coat and walking shoes and set off to Fanny Merryweather's. Her steps were firm and she muttered to herself as she walked, "Plum pudding. Ugh. I feel like a plum pudding. If Fanny has her mother's recipe, she ought to have her pudding mold."

Occasionally a car came past with families on their way to holiday gatherings. No one paid any attention to the tall, straight, elderly woman walking purposefully and mumbling to herself.

When she was almost to Fanny's building, Arletta suddenly remembered that Fanny was spending Christmas with her niece. In the hope that she hadn't left yet, Arletta rang the doorbell. Almost immediately the door opened. Fanny was surprised, "Oh, Arletta, my friend, Arletta. Come in."

"I'm glad I caught you home."

"I'm not hard to find at home."

"I meant I'm glad I caught you before your niece came for you."

A startled look crossed Fanny's round face and then she smiled sadly, "Rather, you caught me in a lie. I have not seen my niece for years. I just like people to think I have somewhere to go for Christmas."

As Fanny's voice drifted off, Arletta asserted herself, "Don't worry about it. You're not the only one who lied. I told everyone I didn't want to go visit my son Dirk and his wife because they make such a fuss over me. Hah! The truth is they didn't invite me. As usual they sent me a check."

Arletta's eyes had turned red and filled with tears. But instead of crying she laughed and the laughter brought the pent-up tears rolling down her cheeks.

When the two women stopped laughing and crying, Arletta explained about the pudding mold. Fanny said she hadn't used the pudding mold in years but it was somewhere. The two women searched through the cupboard and found it, dusty and worse for wear and age but a sure enough pudding mold.

Firmly Arletta took Fanny's arm, "Come on, Fanny. We're going to make this old plum pudding and we're going to eat it. Get your coat on."

The two women laughed and talked as they prepared the food and set the table. When George arrived in his best blue suit and smelling of shaving lotion and hair tonic, the conversation became considerably louder. George smiled and answered even when he didn't exactly hear them right and then they would all laugh together. No one could believe the way Christmas Day was turning out.

The plum pudding was done. With Fanny giving directions, Arletta unmolded the perfect, fragrant pudding onto her white milk-glass serving dish. Arletta was overcome with a strong sense of pride in the spicy-smelling pudding. Polly would be so surprised.

Just then the doorbell rang and Arletta hurried to admit Polly.

"Merry Christmas!" Polly shouted as Arletta opened the door.

Polly was wearing her usual run-down shoes and shabby-looking black coat and leaning heavily on her

With a great show of mystery Polly set the kettle on the kitchen counter.

cane with one hand, but in the other hand she was holding a large, dented kettle by its heavy wire handle. With a great show of mystery Polly sat it on the kitchen counter. Reaching inside the kettle Polly took out a package. With a flourish she deposited it on the table. As they all stared at it Polly proudly proclaimed, "Plum pudding. I made you plum pudding."

Arletta's laugh was almost hysterical as she hugged the beaming but confused Polly. While Fanny helped Polly with her coat, Arletta very quietly lifted her white serving dish with the perfectly shaped plum pudding and put it on the highest shelf in her cupboard well out of sight, then gently closed the door.

As Arletta put Polly's plum pudding on another serving dish, tears rolled down her cheeks. She mumbled, "Merry Christmas, you silly old plum pudding."

Mother Merryweather's Plum Pudding

¼ pound or 1 cup of ground suet
1 cup plus 3 tablespoons brown sugar
½ cup milk
2 well beaten eggs
1 cup seedless raisins
1½ cups currants
⅓ cup sliced preserved orange peel
⅓ cup sliced preserved lemon peel
⅓ cup citron
½ cup chopped blanched almonds
1 cup flour, sifted
1 teaspoon baking soda and 1 teaspoon salt
1 teaspoon cinnamon
¼ teaspoon nutmeg and ¼ teaspoon mace
1 cup soft day-old bread crumbs

Mix together suet, brown sugar, and milk. Add the beaten eggs. Mix the fruits, nuts, and peels with ¼ cup of the flour. Sift together the remaining flour with the soda, salt, and spices. Add fruit mixture, crumbs, and sifted dry ingredients to tightly closed pudding mold. Steam on top of the range 2½ hours. Keep the boiling water to half the depth of the mold. When done, remove and invert on a hot serving dish. Make one for a friend.

They Stitch Up Christmas Molas

MARJORIE VANDERVELDE

A GROUP OF CUNA WOMEN running barefoot down the beach, their red headscarves blowing in the tradewinds, looks as colorful as a flight of jungle butterflies. A tropical sun sparkles on their gold noserings, saucerlike earrings, and bead-wrapped arms and legs. Multiple strings of necklaces (some made of animal teeth and/or old coins) and rings on every finger complete their festive traditional costuming. Nevertheless, the glory of each woman is her mola blouse!

Welcome to the pre-Columbian culture of the Cuna Indians, whose small thatch houses crowd the island of Ailigandi just off the Atlantic coast of Panama. Ailigandi is one of some 300 islands in the San Blas Archipelago, which extends from the Panama Canal to Colombia, South America. Less then 50 of these islands are inhabited, as most lack fresh water. Although the islands are claimed by Panama, they are mostly self-governing. Their social structure consists of extended families overseen by elderly matriarchs, although at the chief level, the men take over.

Up until 1933, scarcely anything from the outside world penetrated the Cuna culture. The Cuna people fiercely isolated themselves. Permission from the chief was needed both in order to leave the island and to enter

it. A tribal law once sentenced to death any outsider found on the island after sunset. In the absence of a written language, the chants of *kantules* bridged the generations and shaped tribal thinking. Tradition also shaped and determined the creation of molas, a fabric art descended from body painting. Traditional art designs, including jungle animals and birds, dominated the molas. Then Christmas came to Ailigandi and even the making of molas changed.

Not everything has changed, however. Molas still are created by the women and girls as they sit in the doorways of their homes, which have stick walls and dirt floors and no windows. Weeks or months may be required to finish the design and intricate stitchery for one mola. With variations, the technique is a reverse applique done on panels of vivid colors. The panels are stacked together and the design sketched on the top layer. The mola maker snips through the layers to whatever color she fancies for that part of the design. The rough edges are then turned under and held firmly with the tiniest of stitches.

Mola designs express the infinite imaginings of the Cuna mind. Still, in that December of 1933, the women gathered curiously around the girl called Chi, wondering what strange design she was snipping with sharp scissors on the panels of her fabric. In time they knew. It was a

left: The Cuna Indians of Ailigandi Island, off the coast of Panama, have created a unique craft form known as molas—reverse appliques done on fabric panels of vivid colors. Many different religious subjects can be seen on Cuna molas, but Christmas scenes, such as this beautifully portrayed nativity, are the most popular.

right: The mola is an important part of the Cuna Indian's traditional dress. This woman is wearing a mola blouse as well as mola anklebands.

far right: This mola depicting an angel was made by a young Cuna Indian girl. Part of the mola-making tradition is to utilize all space, thus creating a vibrant background to complement the subject.

Christmas nativity, showing the stable, Joseph, Mary, the baby Jesus, and stable animals, all intricately stitched on a mola!

How had the story of Christmas entered the life of Ailigandi? It came through one of their own tribe, one who had gone "outside." Lonnie Iglesias, a respected Cuna, had gone "outside" to attend Nyack Missionary Institute in Nyack, New York. There he had met and married Marvel, an American. Lonnie and Marvel then returned to Ailigandi with permission to start a school.

On the first day of school, a blast on a conch shell, in lieu of a bell, brought 90 boys running. They had neither clothes nor names.

Lonnie advised, "They don't know they're naked, why should we tell them? But they do need names."

So the two teachers named the pupils for friends in the United States, then for presidents and queens. Today a Cuna chief is named Franklin D. Roosevelt. There is also a Queen Elizabeth, a George Washington, and a John Kennedy.

Lonnie had no language problem, for he spoke Spanish, English, and Cuna. Marvel, however, only spoke English, so she and her pupils struck an agreement. They would teach her Cuna and she would teach them English, which was the language of the coconut traders. It was a school like no other. In time, girls were allowed to attend also and Bible reading was permitted.

Gathered on the moonlit beach under palm trees strummed by the tradewinds, the Cunas of Ailigandi listened as Lonnie and Marvel related the story of Jesus' birth and they struggled to comprehend its significance. Later, as the men fished the ocean in their *cayucos*, they discussed this strange news. So did the women, sitting in the doorways of their windowless homes and stitching molas. Clearly captivated by these new tales, the girl Chi stitched the story into her new mola, which in turn would be made into a blouse to be worn over her heart.

"Little by little my people are beginning to understand," Lonnie told Marvel. He would read to the people from a Spanish Bible, then translate it into Cuna. But the Cunas began saying, "God must be a Spaniard, since the Bible is in Spanish. And we don't forget what the Spanish gold-seekers did to our ancestors!"

It quickly became clear that a Cuna Bible was needed. With the help of the American Bible Society, the Iglesiases devised a Cuna alphabet and started the slow process of translating the Bible into that language. American Bible Society linguists, Dr. Eugene Nida and Dr. Kenneth Pike, spent some time at the Cuna mission perfecting segment translations. In 1948 the book of Mark was published.

The December came when the Christmas story was read from the Cuna-language Bible, made possible by the newly devised Cuna alphabet! The excitement was overwhelming. "Now we know that the babe in the manger was Cuna!" the people sang out.

Even the chiefs were excited when they saw the book of Mark in Cuna. Along with the other men, they became interested in the Christian message and began attending Christian meetings. Women came too and brought along the molas they were making, stitching away at them as they would do during the weekly meetings at which the chief advises them on how to be good wives and mothers. On another day the men would gather to be advised by the chief on how to be good husbands and fathers.

Now Cunas also gather to read and study the word of God from a complete New Testament in their language. The molas the women wear depict Noah's ark, Jonah and the whale, David and Goliath, along with more traditional subjects. But the Christmas molas are favorites. As the Cunas told Lonnie and Marvel: "We used to mark the years from one iguana season to the next iguana season. Now, we will measure the years from Christmas to Christmas!"

Angels in the Snow

KRISTINE NYMOEN

MOMMA, WHAT DOES an angel look like?" "I don't know!" I don't dare take my eyes from the road. Luke lapses into silence and plays with the strap of his seat belt.

"Stop that!" I order. But I am glad that Sam and I have always insisted that the children wear their belts.

"Angels have wings," I tell him. I can't waste my attention on a better answer.

"Remember," the radio crackles, "if you get stranded stay with your car. You will be found. Whether you stay alive or not depends on using your own good sense." The signal fades in and out. Although the message is important, it is not reassuring. I hit the off button, the glove on my hand muffling the metallic snap.

I don't need to be told to be careful. The muscles in my shoulders are tight as I grip the steering wheel. My forehead is pleated with concentration.

Wind whips across Highway 61. The wipers sweep back and forth, scraping great clouds of snow from the windshield. Headlights are almost useless for guidance through the late afternoon storm, but they at least make my orange station wagon more visible to other traffic. There is only one other vehicle that I am aware of, the semi that's trailing too closely behind us.

Snow angels dance around the hood of the car. They are caught momentarily in the muted headlights before being carried off by the wind.

The snow has filled and distorted everything. I shiver and Luke, thinking I'm cold, reaches over and turns the heater fan to its highest level.

"Thanks, son," I say. But it is fear, not cold, that has me trembling. Oblivious, Luke curls up on the seat and dozes, sure that when he awakes we will be safely home. I wish I had his confidence.

I hunch over the wheel peering into the whirling snow in front of us. I can't distinguish the road from the ditch anymore. I should stop now, right where we are, but I see the lights of the semi briefly in the rearview mirror. The heavy Monson truck is running as blindly as I am. Would the driver be able to avoid hitting us on the slick road? I bite my lip and search the whiteness in front of me for indications of the highway.

White-outs are uncommon in Minnesota, occurring just often enough to impress tourists who think of the state as the American Siberia. This is the kind of storm that built that legend.

This morning it was crisp. The air was deceptively calm. The only cloud was the long gray mass that followed the shore of Lake Superior. I had listened to the weather report on the radio and, trusting in radar, made the 113 mile trip from Grand Marais to Duluth. Luke's eye appointment had been set for a month and it would have been difficult to reschedule.

At 1:15 when the optometrist fitted Luke's glasses and we started back home to Grand Marais there was only the slightest hint of snow in the air. The wind started to pick up as we neared Two Harbors. Now, at 4:30 in the afternoon we still have 40 miles to go. At my current speed this won't take more than four or five hours.

Luke's head nods. He sleeps with his new glasses clutched possessively in his left hand. At home Sam will be anxious. I visualize him nervously going to the window, listening for the sound of my car.

I should have stayed in Silver Bay, I tell myself with crystal clear hindsight. The State Troopers pulled in the snowplows 15 minutes ago. The announcement had come over the radio. But they didn't say what to do if you were in the middle of nowhere, with not a house or building visible to offer shelter.

I don't dare stop. There are too many stories of drivers following each others' tracks right into the ditch. I glance quickly into the mirror. The truck is lost in the storm but I feel its ominous presence like a hand pushing me from behind.

Bleached afternoon light manages to penetrate the clouds and lighten the storm. But daylight won't last much longer.

Steering by instinct I inch the car along, feeling for the shoulder. On my right I can hear Lake Superior roaring in the grip of the wind. Within 50 yards of the highway, 10-foot waves crash against basalt cliffs and are slapped back into the face of the wind. But it is invisible to me. The storm has come like a huge eraser, leaving only the blank vortex of snow a few feet in front of me.

Cautiously I ease left, sensing that I've strayed from the center of the road. "Broad is the road that leads to . . ." To what? I can't remember the rest of the Bible verse that Miss Henderson worked so hard to teach me when my parents dropped me off at Sunday school.

Through the soles of my feet I feel a change in the texture of the highway's surface. "Too far!" a voice inside me cries. "You've gone too far!" I pull the wheel over hard to the right. The station wagon fishtails, and I feath-

The storm has come like a huge eraser, leaving only a blank vortex of snow a few feet in front of me.

er the brakes trying to control the skid. We slide noiselessly for about 30 feet as I pump futilely at the brake. With the sudden shock of impact Luke and I are jammed forward against our seat belts then snapped back hard into our seats. The hood crumples as the car is enfolded in the arms of a big spruce tree.

We stop with a jerk. "Destruction," I remember with sudden clarity. "Broad is the road to destruction."

Through the window I can see the needles of the black spruce pushing tight against the windshield. I can hear the sound of the branches scraping at the car trying to get inside. Gray light comes in the back and side windows that extend beyond the tree's embrace.

The car brightens briefly in the lights from the monster semi. I grab for Luke and hold my breath until the truck lumbers past. Exhaling I collapse against the back of the seat. It didn't hit us, but the driver isn't going to see us and stop to help either.

Luke rubs his temple gingerly, his eyes wide, not entirely sure that he isn't still dreaming. "Are we stuck?" he asks, disapproval heavy in his voice. He slips on his glasses, the gesture still uncomfortable and new. They don't help. The view, as he strains to see over the dash, is of the broken limbs of the tree.

"I'm afraid so, honey." I try not to sound worried. The car already seems colder as I shift rapidly from forward to reverse trying to create a rocking motion that will allow me to back onto the highway. Even as I go through the motions I know the effort is wasted.

After five minutes of spinning the wheels I give up. Luke looks frightened when I switch off the motor to conserve gas. The storm and the tree have blocked most of the afternoon sunlight, but I can see the vertical line that marks Luke's forehead when worried.

I reach over the back of the car seat and retrieve his red stocking cap. "Better put this on," I say.

He slips the cap over his ears and zips up his ski jacket.

"Don't worry, honey," I tell him, sounding surprisingly calm. "We're just stuck. The plow will be along in a while. It's not even cold." Not yet anyway, but the weather report predicted a low of minus 15, with rising winds.

"I want to show Colleen my new glasses before she goes to bed," he says petulantly.

"We'll probably be home by then," I answer, trying to suppress my nervous irritation. "In the meantime you get out the survival kit you made." It's a mistake. Luke's eyes open wide, or maybe it's just a distortion caused by his new glasses.

"Sure, momma." His voice is subdued. He unstraps his seat belt and I dodge his old boots as he jackknifes over the back of the seat.

Why did I start out without blankets in the back? I ask myself, helpless now to change things.

Luke lifts the carpet and, reaching into the space beside the spare tire, brings out the three pound coffee can that he filled in Sunday school and gave Sam and me for Christmas. I try to remember the contents.

As Luke proudly hands me the kit, then pulls himself back over the seat, I think of all the things I've heard about staying alive in a blizzard. I also remember the stories about the people who have died. Unfortunately that brings up the prospect of hypothermia. Hypother-

mia is caused when the body cools below a certain point and can't warm itself. We have to stay warm and dry.

We spread the contents of the can on the seat between us. There is a ragged red streamer of cloth, a scrubby

We spread the contents of the can on the seat between us. There is a ragged red streamer of cloth, a scrubby chunk of candle stuck in an old tuna can, a foil-wrapped package of matches, and five packages of raisins.

chunk of candle stuck into an old tuna can, a foil-wrapped package of matches, and five tiny packages of raisins.

I take the strip of cloth and the coffee can from him. The door on the driver's side is pinned shut by the tree so I wedge myself over the back of the seat and force a rear door open. It leaves a half circle in the snow like the wings of the snow angels I used to make when I was little. I feel the temperature drop as soon as I get out, and my cheeks start to burn. Wind catches the door and slams it shut behind me.

Holding my gloved hand over my mouth and nose, I fight my way around the car to tie the red rag onto the corner of the roof rack. I hurry, spurred on by the wind. The snow comes up past my knees, turning my high black boots into scoops that take up the cold and hold it next to me. I cough a few times and squint as my eyes tear up. If there is a plow still out they might see us. But the light is fading fast.

With the coffee can I scoop away the soft, unsettled snow from around the tail pipe. Snow clings to my glove and chafes the naked band of skin at my wrists. I scrape out a trench a few inches deep then walk back toward the door.

In the deep, heavy snow each step is an effort and an act of faith. There are no hillocks to tell me where footing is safe and where it is treacherous. I slip. Some branch buried beneath the surface has rolled me onto my shoulder. Damp white powder coats my clothing.

Don't get wet! That is the primary rule of survival, and I have broken it.

"Mommy, are you all right?" Luke opens his door and jumps out into the snow.

"Get back in the car!" My voice is sharp. He retreats like a frightened turtle and the door closes as I struggle up on one knee.

Back inside I strip off Luke's jacket and shake the snow off of his clothes. His nylon jacket and ski pants shed the snow before it has time to melt. His boots are second-hand but extra warm. I brush off his legs and try not to scold. My own blue jeans are wet to the thighs, but there is nothing I can do about it.

Luke's thumb is in his mouth—something he hasn't done since Colleen was born two years ago.

We clamber, one at a time, into the front seat and I take him into my arms. "Don't worry, honey. We'll be all right," I reassure him.

I turn on the engine, timing it carefully. Ten minutes of warmth every half hour and carbon monoxide won't reach dangerous levels.

There isn't any twilight. Darkness comes as suddenly as a frosty breath vanishing in the wind.

"It's time to light the candle," Luke says authoritatively.

"No, honey," I explain, "that's to keep us warm later." One lit candle is supposed to provide enough warmth to keep us from freezing to death.

"Well, then turn on the car light."

I am tempted, but again I must desist. "No honey, we don't want to run down the battery. We need to be able to start the car to keep us warm."

"Well then, start the car. I'm cold," he says plaintively.

"I can't do that either. We have to be careful about too much carbon monoxide getting into the car." I try to maintain my patience. Sam is better at this than I am. I wish he were with me. But he's not. "Come over here by me and we'll keep each other warm," I suggest.

Luke snuggles close and I put my arm around him.

"How much longer do you think it will be, mom?"

"Soon, dear," I say, hoping it's the truth. "Why don't we play a game?"

We start with the rhyming game. Luke says a word and I think of a rhyme.

"Snow, " be begins.

"Blow," I respond.

"Toe," he answers.

"Tow truck." A telling remark, I realize.

"Stuck," Luke says after a long thoughtful pause.

"Let's do something else," I say in my best mother-has-an-idea voice.

"O.K." Luke says. "Let's eat the raisins. I'm hungry." He turns the package over in his hands and studies the picture of the girl in the red bonnet. "Are we gonna freeze, mom?"

I turn on the overhead light and look down into his blue eyes. "No, dear. We'll be fine." I don't want him to panic. I have a momentary inspiration. "Do you want to ask God to help us?"

"You don't believe that stuff, do you?" he asks.

I guess I shouldn't be shocked, but I am. When Luke turned six, Sam and I decided our son needed to learn about God. So a few months ago we began leaving him at Sunday school while we went out for brunch. Miss Henderson is still there, spreading her love to children.

"Don't you believe it?" I ask, my voice carefully neutral.

"Come on, mom!" For a moment he sounds like a teenager. "Miss Henderson tells us all these stories with magic and angels. Have you ever seen an angel?"

"No," I admit. Is the car getting colder? The upholstery feels stiff beneath me.

"That's because there aren't any."

Glad of the distraction Luke provides, I think back to my days in Sunday school. "Have you learned about Moses?" I ask.

Luke nods. "You mean the baby in the basket?"

"That's the one. When Moses grew up he saw God."

Luke's warm breath tickles my cheek. Moisture condenses on the windows and turns to frost. It coats the chrome trim as I tell the story of the commandments the way I remember hearing it—like Miss Henderson told it to me.

"So Moses got ready to climb the mountain and see what God had to say to him. But God said, 'Be careful. If you look right into my face, the glory of my countenance—that's like face—will kill you.' So Moses went up the mountain and got the commandments and he saw God but he was careful not to look right at God's face."

"So what did he look like, mom?"

"Well the Bible didn't say exactly. It only said that God was glorious and that he told Moses not to look right at him."

"Yah, I'll bet." Luke says. "Anyway, that's God. What does an angel look like?"

I can feel him shivering as he talks. "The Bible described an angel as a person dressed in clothing whiter than snow." I look out at the drift that is in the process of covering the side windows.

"You mean dazzling-brilliant-sunny white, like the soap commercials?"

I can see that my venture into theology is doomed. "Yes," I say.

"Did God say to go to church?" Luke asks and I know what is coming.

There is nothing to see, nothing to do. I start to talk, at first only to stay awake, but then it becomes a kind of prayer.

"Yes, Luke, you have to go to Sunday school. Everybody has to go to Sunday school."

"You don't," he persists.

"But I'm grown up," I try to explain.

"As soon as I'm grown up I'm not going either," he declares. He starts to draw with his finger in the frost on the window until I turn off the light and tell him to try to sleep.

Every half hour I run the car for ten minutes. By midnight snow has snaked into the ignition system and the car won't start. The stubby candle is all we have for warmth. I gauge the length to the final millimeter. But no matter how I calculate, it won't last the night.

As Luke naps I play mind games. I will not fall asleep and let death creep up like a thief.

"What does an angel look like?" I ask myself. White robes, I suppose. Wings. I seem to remember one of Miss Henderson's stories that mentioned more than one set. Two pair? I ask myself. That seems unbalanced. Three, I decide. Three pairs of wings and robes of white. Most everyone who saw them was frightened, so I add an unworldly shimmer to my mental picture.

Snow continues to drift. I light the candle at intervals, and the frost on the window above it melts into sooty tear drops. I blow it out and stare into the dark, trying not to think about the cold that is creeping up my wet legs. Luke will be fine, I tell myself. The sound of the wind is muffled by the drifts now.

There is nothing to see, nothing to do. Feeling a little foolish I start to talk, at first only to stay awake, but then it becomes a kind of prayer. After a while it seems like someone is right there in the front seat beside Luke and me. And I feel like God is watching over us.

Luke moves in my arms. "My feet went to sleep," he whines. That isn't too surprising considering the cramped quarters.

My hands tremble with cold as I set him beside me and turn on the light. His face is a shock. His lips are blue. I snatch up the matches on the dash and light the candle.

I take off his boots, something I should have done as soon as we got back in the car. His socks are soaked through. The dye from the inside of his boots has stained them gray in patches. I yank the socks from his feet and cup his numb toes in my hands.

Pulling out my shirttail, I hold his feet against the warmth of my flesh. How cold they are! Luke lies limp on the seat looking up at me.

"Flap your arms, Luke," I order. "Flap your arms like you're trying to fly. We have to get you warm."

He moves his arms in a desultory fashion.

"Luke, you can't go back to sleep!" I lean over him and force him to swing his arms up and down. "Wake up, Luke! Sing!"

"Jingle bells, jingle bells," he starts tiredly.

"That's right, sing!" I join in, "Jingle all the way." But there is a catch in my voice and I have to stop.

"You know that one, mom."

"Yes, honey, I remember. Do you know any songs with motions?"

"You mean like 'Itsy Bitsy Spider'?"

"Yes, let's do that one."

"But that's a baby song."

"I don't care. Just do it." We sing loud and off-key with Luke's toes pressed against my midriff. And between songs I talk and pray and keep Luke moving. I make him eat the last of the raisins, calling it breakfast though it is only four o'clock.

He is tired and shivering most of the time now, great shudders that neither one of us know how to stop and that do nothing to warm him. Desperate, I unbutton my shirt and wrap him up close next to my heart.

Back and forth we rock, trying to keep warm. The candle dies. It couldn't have lasted. And it is against all logic to have expected God to hear me and answer my prayers. But I hate God then, hate the false hope, the broken promise. And I hate myself for putting my son in danger.

Luke mutters incoherently, saying he is hot. I hold him tight refusing to let him out of my embrace, loving him even though he fights me.

"God, send us an angel," I demand, no longer content to beg.

Luke quiets in my arms, a frightening calm. There isn't much time left. He needs to be warmed quickly.

I set him down and pull a few crumpled kleenex from my pocket. I stuff them into the tuna can candleholder and scratch one of the precious matches against the dash. The paper flares briefly as I dig under the seat for something else to burn. There are a couple of Hershey bar wrappers and an old road map. I feed the map into the flame a section at a time until it is gone and I have watched the last of the sparks die.

Taking Luke back into my arms I wrap him next to my skin and peace settles over us like a blanket of snow. I don't trust it. It is just the cold. But the peace stays, calming my building hysteria. I sleep.

Screech, screech. I start awake at the sound. A shovel scrapes against the glass as someone clears the drift from the rear window. Light temporarily blinds me but I see a form in outline.

"They're alive!" someone shouts.

I hug Luke close.

The road crew pulls us out through the window and wraps us in their own jackets, which smell like gasoline and sweat.

I ride into town in the snowplow, squeezed between the two men with Luke in my lap, the heater on high, and the gear shift between my knees. The men grin every time they look at us, alive. Sam has had them searching for us up and down the shore since dawn, but it was the tattered red pennant tied on the roof rack that attracted their attention. That was all of the car that was visible from the road.

But what does an angel look like?

Miss Henderson would be surprised at my answer:

Angels? They wear chopper mitts and heavy caps with fur earlaps pulled down. They could use a shave and their teeth aren't straight, but the glory of their countenance is blinding.

I determine to tell Miss Henderson what I've learned, next Sunday in church.

Our Christmas

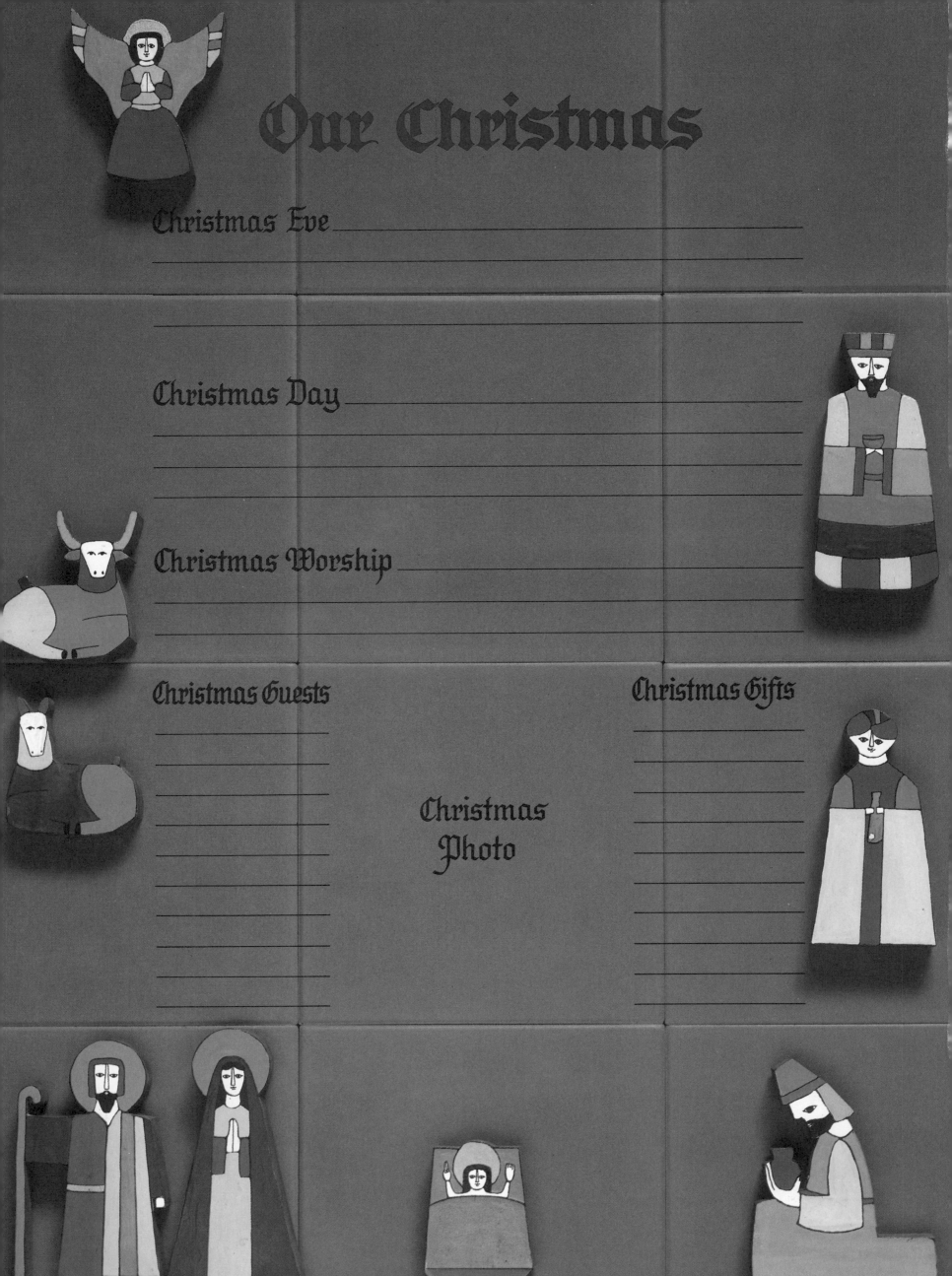

Christmas Eve _____
_____

Christmas Day _____
_____
_____

Christmas Worship _____
_____
_____

Christmas Guests
_____
_____
_____
_____
_____
_____
_____
_____

Christmas Gifts
_____
_____
_____
_____
_____
_____
_____
_____

Christmas
Photo

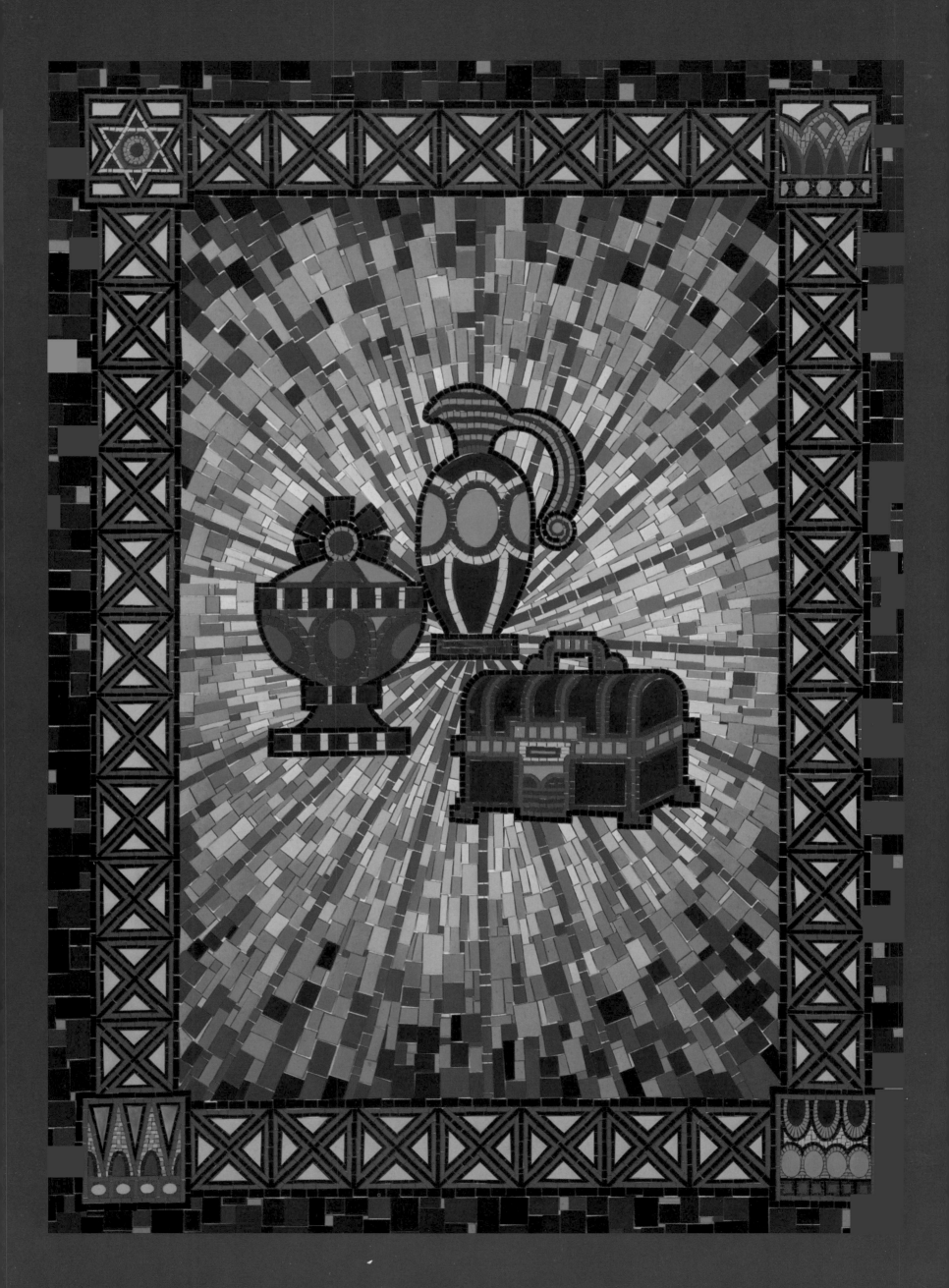